COLD WAR

1946 to 1991

First published in July 2016

A catalogue record for this book is available from the British Library.

ISBN 978 1 78521 053 2

Library of Congress control no. 2015958625

Published by Haynes Publishing,
Sparkford, Yeovil,
Somerset BA22 7JJ, UK.
Tel: 01963 440635
Int. tel: +44 1963 440635
Website: www.haynes.co.uk

Haynes North America Inc.,
861 Lawrence Drive, Newbury Park,
California 91320, USA.

Printed in Malaysia.

Copy editor: Michelle Tilling
Proof reader: Penny Housden
Indexer: Peter Nicholson
Page design: James Robertson

COLD WAR

1946 to 1991

Operations Manual

Insights into surviving ideological conflict,
mutual assured destruction, and the nuclear apocalypse

Pat Ware

Contents

FALLOUT SHELTER

'I do not believe that civilisation will be wiped out in a war fought with the atomic bomb. Perhaps two-thirds of the people of the earth will be killed.'

Albert Einstein, 1879–1955

Introduction

The expression 'Cold War' describes a period of military and political tension between East and West that existed from 1946 to 1991. Although the term had first been used by George Orwell in an article entitled 'You and the Atom Bomb' published in the *Tribune* in October 1945, it entered the common culture following a speech given by the American statesman Bernard Baruch.

Addressing the South Carolina House of Representatives in April 1947, Baruch said 'Let us not be deceived … we are today in the midst of a cold war … our enemies are to be found abroad and at home … let us never forget this … our unrest is the heart of their success. The peace of the world is the hope and the goal of our political system … it is the despair and defeat of those who stand against us.'

Six months later, at a Senate Special Committee investigating the National Defense Program, Baruch returned to the theme, stating that 'although the shooting war is over, we are in the midst of a cold war which is getting warmer'. On one side of this Cold War were the Western powers that would form the North Atlantic Treaty Organization (NATO); on the other was the Soviet Union and the satellite states of the Warsaw Pact.

The Cold War brought an end to the uneasy

ABOVE The Berlin Wall, constructed during 1961, came to signify the divide between East and West. This photograph was taken at the junction of Elsen Strasse and Heidelberger Strasse in the American sector. *(Warehouse Collection)*

alliance that had seen the Soviet Union join with Britain, Canada and the USA in 1941 to defeat Germany and Japan. Cracks in the alliance had started to emerge in May 1945, following the German surrender, and were exacerbated by the USA's use of atomic weapons in Japan. The Soviet Union consolidated its hold over East Germany and over countries such as Poland, Hungary and Czechoslovakia, and soon an 'Iron Curtain' separated East and West. In

June 1948, the Soviets blocked access to the Western-controlled areas of Berlin in an attempt to bring the entire city under Soviet control. A huge Allied airlift was established, delivering 300 tons of food, fuel and other necessities every day into Berlin Tempelhof airport. The West's determination ensured that the Soviet gamble failed and, in May 1949, the blockade was lifted, and Germany was divided into two separate states with competing ideologies – the German Democratic Republic (GDR) in the east, and the Federal Republic of Germany (DDR) in the west.

In August 1949, the Soviet Union carried out its first test of a fission device, breaking the US monopoly in atomic weapons and heralding the beginning of the nuclear arms race. Not long after, Britain also joined the 'nuclear club', although it was often difficult to separate the nation's 'independent nuclear deterrent' from the arsenal of 'the American cousins'. Other nations, including China, France, India, Pakistan, Israel and North Korea have subsequently developed nuclear weapons.

In 1950, in a pamphlet entitled 'Survival under Atomic Attack', the US government stated that 'atomic weapons will not destroy the earth … not even hydrogen bombs will blow the earth apart or kill us all by radioactivity'. Nevertheless, during three decades, the two sides struggled to acquire nuclear supremacy. Despite attempts at reaching agreement on arms control, ever-more monstrous sums of money were committed to the acquisition of weapons that could destroy civilisation many times over. Similar sums were devoted to espionage, to so-called 'early warning' systems, and to devising and building the insane infrastructure required to support the very notion of nuclear war.

For 50 years, the world stood uneasily on the edge of nuclear warfare, with few doubting that, should the Cold War turn hot, neither side could emerge victorious. The first chink of light came in the mid- to late 1980s, when, in an attempt to control military expenditure, President Gorbachev refused to commit Soviet troops to support the failing Warsaw Pact regimes in Eastern Europe. A wave of revolutions saw the old order overturned in one Soviet bloc country after another, including the GDR, and,

RIGHT Operation Buster Jangle was a series of seven nuclear tests conducted at the Nevada Test Site in 1951. The largest weapon was a 31-kiloton bomb, code-named 'Dog', whilst 'Charlie', seen here, yielded 14 kilotons. *(US National Nuclear Security Administration)*

on 3 October 1990, East and West Germany were unified. Within three weeks 22 nations had signed the Conventional Forces in Europe Treaty, limiting the numbers of troops and weapons that could be held by the two sides in Europe. In December 1991, following a power struggle in Moscow, the Soviet Union collapsed.

Most historians would agree that the Cold War was now well and truly over.

Nevertheless, even 25 years later, the Cold War, along with the very real, though curiously farcical, threat of nuclear apocalypse, remains a potent force in popular culture, and, of course, the worldwide nuclear stockpiles also remain – diminished, but more than capable of destroying civilisation. It seems that the world must continue to 'live under the shadow of the bomb'.

'Considering how likely we all are to be blown to pieces by it within the next five years, the atomic bomb has not roused so much discussion as might have been expected.'

**George Orwell,
'You and the Atomic Bomb', October 1945**

Chapter One

The Cold War story

Although it symbolises the military tensions of the nuclear age, the Cold War was primarily a conflict of ideologies rather than weapons. The technology simply provided a measure of the competition between the two sides. However, the fear of unleashing the nuclear apocalypse – a possible complete or near-complete annihilation of life on the planet by the use of a large enough quantity of nuclear weapons – almost certainly prevented the two sides engaging one another.

OPPOSITE **The ruins of Nagasaki Temple photographed in September 1946, some six weeks after the attack on the city.** *(Corporal Lynn P. Walker, Jr; US Department of Defense)*

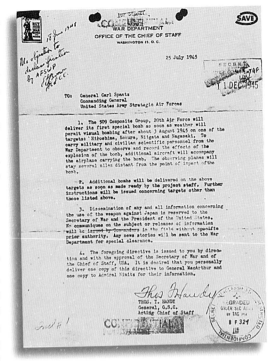

The world awoke to the realities of the nuclear
age on 6 August 1945 when a lone B-29
Superfortress bomber of the US Army Air Force,
piloted by Paul Tibbets and Robert Lewis,
and named 'Enola Gay' in dubious honour of
Tibbets's mother, dropped a primitive atomic
bomb on the Japanese port city of Hiroshima.
The target was selected on the basis that it had
not been previously bombed, and thus it would
be easier to assess the scale of damage. The
B-29 took off from Tinian Island, approximately
1,500 miles (2,430km) south of Tokyo, and

approached the city at a height of 30,000ft
(9,150m). Releasing the bomb two miles (3km)
short of the target, the aircraft immediately veered
away, returning at a height of 28,500ft (8,695m).
A handwritten note on the pilot's flight log, which
was recently offered for sale at auction, warned
that the aircraft must 'stay at least 2–3 miles from
the atomic cloud at all times'.

For maximum destructive effect, the
15-kiloton fission bomb, code-named 'Little
Boy', was exploded at a height of less than
2,000ft (655m). The bomb contained about
140lb (64kg) of enriched uranium, an extremely
dense, purple-black metal. Despite the fact that
only a tiny proportion of this material actually
fissioned, the temperature on the ground
directly beneath the blast reached 10,000°F
(5,500°C), and a cloud of debris rose 11 miles
(18km) into the air. One square mile of the city
was wiped out, and 90% of buildings were
destroyed within a radius of 4.4 square miles
(11km²). Firefighting was rendered impossible
by the fact that 26 out of 33 fire stations were
destroyed; water, electricity and gas utilities
were severely disrupted, and all of the city's
hospitals were damaged. Glass was broken at
a distance of almost 8 miles (13km) from the
centre of the explosion.

The fact that the bomb was released by a lone
aircraft had the effect of increasing the death toll;
the aircraft was not determined to be a threat
and the city's air-raid warning was cancelled.
Of the city's population of around 300,000, the

ABOVE Mushroom cloud photographed by the tail-gunner of 'Enola Gay', Staff-Sergeant George R. (Bob) Caron, at 20,000ft (6,100m) above Hiroshima after the dropping of 'Little Boy'. *(US National Archives)*

ABOVE RIGHT Hiroshima, after the bomb. *(US Department of Defense)*

authorities estimated that around one-quarter were killed immediately by the initial explosion and the ensuing wave of intense heat, whilst a similar number were injured. The overall casualty figure included 260 doctors out of a total of 300, 1,800 nurses out of 2,400 and some 80% of the firemen on duty. Deaths from the effects of radiation continued for many years after.

Making an entry in his log on his return from the mission, co-pilot Captain Robert Lewis wrote: 'My God, what have we done', and one contemporary journal described the bomb as 'the world's most terrifying weapon'. Not

RIGHT Now described as the Hiroshima Peace Memorial or the Genbaku Dome, the ruins of the Hiroshima Prefectural Industrial Promotion Hall survive to this day as a monument to those who died at Hiroshima. *(Frank 'Fg2' Gualtieri)*

ABOVE Mushroom cloud over Nagasaki as a result of the detonation of 'Fat Man', the second atomic bomb. The name was a reference to the bomb's distinctive rounded shape. (US National Archives)

BELOW Atomic cloud over Nagasaki, seen from neighbouring Koyagi-jima Island; 9 August 1945. (Hiromichi Matsuda)

everyone shared Lewis's horror. For example, Henry Stimson, US Secretary of War, said that the bomb had been intended to 'make a profound psychological impression on as many inhabitants [of Japan] as possible'. President Harry S. Truman described it as the 'bomb to end bombs', and made the following public announcement after the raid: 'Sixteen hours ago an American aeroplane dropped one bomb on Hiroshima, Japan. That bomb had more power than 20,000 tons of TNT and more than 2,000 times the blast power of the British "grand slam", which [at 22,000lb] is the largest bomb yet used in the history of warfare.' Speaking after the event, General Carl Spaatz, US Commander of the Strategic Air Forces in the Pacific, told journalists that he believed that had the 'new bomb' been developed earlier it would have shortened the war in Europe, and may even have obviated the need for the D-Day invasion and the slog across France into Germany.

But the Japanese failed to surrender immediately, apparently refusing to believe that the USA had constructed a nuclear bomb, or, if such a feat had been achieved, that there could not have been more than a single weapon available. Three days later, on 9 August 1945, a second nuclear device, code-named 'Fat Man' in reference to its rounded shape, was dropped on Nagasaki. The original target had been Kitakyushu, but the city was obscured by heavy cloud, and the lone Superfortress, nicknamed 'Bockscar' after its usual pilot, Captain Frederick C. Bock, was diverted to Nagasaki. The pilot given the dubious honour of carrying out this particular mission was Major Charles W. Sweeney.

'Fat Man' had a yield of 21 kilotons, and was based on plutonium-239, using an implosion technology. The bomb was detonated 1,625ft (500m) directly above a suburb that included factories, housing and schools, destroying 2.6 square miles (6.7m²) of the city; 23% of the city's 51,000 buildings were either razed to the ground by blast, or were burned. The harbour and the residential areas escaped serious damage, but the huge Mitsubishi factory in the Urakami Valley was destroyed. There was no firestorm, but the column of smoke and debris could be seen more than 250 miles

(405km) away. Of the city's population of around 270,000, the Committee on Damage by Atomic Bombs in Hiroshima and Nagasaki estimated that 75,000 were killed immediately by the initial explosion and intense heat, whilst a further 75,000 were injured.

The Americans believed that, within two weeks, they would be in a position to drop a third bomb on Japan, with the cities of Osaka, Nagoya and Yokosuka listed as possible targets. However, Japan surrendered unconditionally on 15 August, signalling the end of the Second World War.

Nuclear weapon development

The notion of nuclear weapons was not new. As early as 1902, two British scientists, Ernest Rutherford, a Scottish Calvinist, and Professor Frederick Soddy, had concluded that atoms contained enormous stores of energy and that, if harnessed, this energy could be used as a formidable weapon. By 1920, scientists had deduced that such a weapon could be based on the fusion of light atoms or the fission – breaking apart – of heavy atoms, and in 1932, James Chadwick, who had been a pupil of Rutherford, discovered the neutron, demonstrating how it could easily be used to penetrate atomic nuclei. Two years later, German chemists Otto Hahn and Fritz Strassmann investigated the effects of bombarding uranium-235, the most complex of the naturally occurring elements, with neutrons. By the end of 1938, Hahn reported in the science journal *Naturwissenschaften* that, under bombardment, the nucleus could be seen to 'burst' or fission and that this produced new elements, including barium, krypton and strontium, plus a very large amount of energy. Clearly, if a chain reaction could be created, then the amount of energy released would be considerable – and if enough uranium were used then it would be possible to harness this energy to produce a bomb with huge destructive power.

A major problem was the availability of sufficient uranium-235, as tons of ore, in the form of pitchblende, were required to produce just a small quantity. The more common

isotope, uranium-238, contains about 0.75% uranium-235 and centrifuges were used to separate out the lighter material. Using the still secret man-made element plutonium-239 was similarly difficult, since the material had to be created in a nuclear reactor.

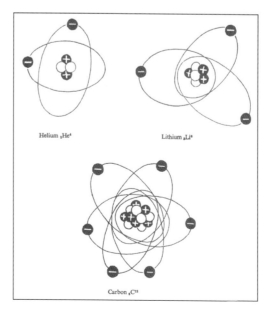

Helium $_2$He^4 Lithium $_3$Li^6

Carbon $_6$C^{12}

ABOVE 'Fat Man' on its transport carriage, photographed at Tinian Island prior to deployment. *(US Department of Defense)*

LEFT A total of around 120 'Fat Man' weapons were manufactured between 1947 and 1949, and the bomb was declared obsolete by 1950. A number of US museums exhibit 'Fat Man' replicas, including the National Museum of the USAF at Dayton, Ohio, and the National Museum of Nuclear Science & History, Albuquerque. *(US Department of Defense)*

LEFT Graphical representation of the structure of atoms. *(Warehouse Collection)*

ABOVE Wartime signboard at Oak Ridge Laboratory, Tennessee. Nicknamed 'the atomic city', the town of Oak Ridge was declared a military district in July 1943 and was surrounded by guard towers and fences. It was here that the Y-12 plant was used to separate uranium-235 from uranium-238 for the Manhattan Project. *(Atomic Heritage Foundation)*

ABOVE Technical area at the Manhattan Project where the atomic bomb was developed. Established in 1942, the project eventually employed more than 130,000 people, and cost nearly US$2 billion at 1945 prices. *(Los Alamos Scientific Laboratory)*

Word of what had been done in Germany soon reached Britain, the Soviet Union and the USA. In 1940, a committee of British scientists was established to report on the present state of knowledge regarding the construction of a nuclear weapon. In September 1941, a new division of the Department of Scientific and Industrial Research was created under the code name 'Tube Alloys', and work started on separating uranium isotopes. At this point, Chadwick believed that Britain was the world

leader in atomic weapons research, and visiting American scientists Professors G.B. Pegram and Harold C. Urey were impressed with what had been achieved, convincing the US government to create a similar project.

The American nuclear programme started in 1942 using the cover name 'Development of substitute materials'. Huge sums of money were allocated to what was really a search for the creation of a practical atomic weapon, and the total cost was eventually close to $2 billion.

Based at the Los Alamos National Laboratory, New Mexico, the work came to be known as the Manhattan Project. The programme was directed by Major General Leslie R. Groves of the US Corps of Engineers, with theoretical physicist J. Robert Oppenheimer as the scientific director. At its height, the Manhattan Project employed more than 130,000 people, and research and production took place at over 30 sites

LEFT Operators at calutron control panels at the Oak Ridge Y-12 plant. Designed by Ernest O. Lawrence during the Manhattan Project, the calutron was a mass spectrometer for separating isotopes of uranium. *(American Museum of Science and Energy)*

across the USA, Britain and Canada. Many scientists and workers from the British project were transferred to the USA. The project was considered to be so secret that even Vice-President Truman was not briefed on the development until 25 April 1945, two weeks after succeeding Roosevelt.

There was initially some doubt as to whether sufficient uranium would be available, but, by November, weapons-grade uranium-235 was being produced at the Y-12 National Security Complex at Oak Ridge, Tennessee, whilst plutonium-239 was manufactured at Hanford, Washington. In May 1945, a quantity of German uranium was captured following the country's surrender.

Towards the end of 1942, scientists at the Metallurgical Laboratory at the University of Chicago had achieved criticality – the term used to describe a perfect balance between the rate of production and loss of neutrons – in a nuclear reactor, allowing two types of atomic bomb to be developed. The first was a relatively simple gun-type fission weapon using enriched uranium-235, as typified by 'Little Boy', whilst the second was a more complex implosion-type weapon based on irradiated and transmuted plutonium. The first atomic test was carried out on 16 July 1945 in the New Mexico desert at

White Sands, about 250 miles (400km) from Los Alamos. Code-named 'Trinity', the implosion-type bomb – described by the scientists as 'the gadget' – produced an explosive power equivalent to about 20 kilotons of TNT.

BELOW Described as 'the gadget', this plutonium-based implosion-fission device was detonated during the 'Trinity' test on 16 July 1945, yielding a TNT equivalent of 20 tons. This was the world's first nuclear explosion. *(US Department of Defense)*

ABOVE During the 'Trinity' test, it was originally planned that 'the gadget' would be placed inside this steel flask to contain the TNT explosion if the nuclear chain reaction failed to materialise. Nicknamed 'Jumbo', the 25ft (7.6m) long flask measured 10ft (3m) in diameter and weighed 214 tons (217 tonnes). *(US Department of Defense)*

ABOVE RIGHT Increasing confidence in the weapon allowed the scientists to abandon the notion of placing 'the gadget' in the steel flask and 'Jumbo' was suspended from a steel tower to be exposed to the effects of the atomic blast. The tower was destroyed, but 'Jumbo' survived intact. *(US Department of Defense)*

RIGHT Robert Oppenheimer and Leslie Groves, photographed after the 'Trinity' test, beside the remains of the tower from which 'Jumbo' was suspended. *(US Department of Defense)*

At the Potsdam Conference in July 1945, Truman was told of the successful 'Trinity' test and, in his diary, he wrote: 'We have discovered the most terrible bomb in the history of the world. It may be the fire destruction prophesied in the Euphrates Valley Era, after Noah and his fabulous Ark.' It was at Potsdam that Truman first told Stalin of the work that the Allies had been doing. Despite the Soviet Union's status as the third major partner in the wartime alliance, neither the USA nor Britain trusted Stalin's intentions so he had previously supposedly been kept in the dark; since he had spies deep in the Manhattan Project, however, he was perfectly aware of what was going on. Truman told Stalin that the Allies were planning to use this weapon on the Japanese to bring the war in the Pacific to an abrupt end, thus obviating the need for invasion. A plan to first mount a demonstration of the bomb which might dissuade the Japanese from continuing to fight was discounted since it would 'waste' one of the only two atomic weapons that were available, so, during August 1945, bombs were dropped on the Japanese cities of Hiroshima and Nagasaki.

Although the USA remains the only nation to have deployed nuclear weapons, President Harry Truman believed that this action shortened the war and saved American lives. In August 1963, in a letter to the Chicago *Sun Times*, Truman defended his approval of the use of the bomb, claiming that it had 'saved 125,000 youngsters on the American side, and 125,000 on the Japanese side from getting killed … [as well as] saving a half million

youngsters on both sides from being maimed for life'. But Gar Alperovitz, founder of the Democracy Collaborative, writing in his book *Atomic Diplomacy*, suggested that there was an alternative reason for the US attacks on Hiroshima and Nagasaki. Although the scale of the attacks convinced Japan that it was futile to continue with the war, the bombs also demonstrated American military might to the Soviet Union.

There is no doubt that its nuclear capability gave the USA enormous power. Brien McMahon, the US Senator for Connecticut, described the bomb as 'the most important thing in history since the birth of Jesus Christ', whilst Arthur H. Compton, a leading US physicist and member of the Manhattan Project, even went so far as to say 'atomic power is ours and who can deny that it was God's will that we should have it'. Whilst Compton may have actually believed that this was true, it soon became clear that the development of nuclear weapons was something of a double-edged sword. There was considerable popular pressure to place the weapons under the control of the newly formed United Nations (UN), and, by spring 1946, the UN Atomic Energy Commission stated that it wished to eliminate all nuclear weapons. The USA countered, presenting a plan which allowed it to control all aspects of nuclear technology – the Soviets disagreed and presented their own proposal for nuclear disarmament. Neither plan was accepted by the UN.

By July 1946, the USA had already conducted its first post-war test. Operation

ABOVE LEFT A nuclear explosion produces an unimaginable combination of heat, blast and light. The fireball is sufficiently intense that even the modest 'Trinity' test produced a glassy residue on the desert floor, consisting of sand, quartz and feldspar that had been melted by the bomb and fused together. This residue was known as Trinitite, Atomsite or Alamogordo Glass. *(US Department of Defense)*

ABOVE The maximum size of the distinctive fireball, and the period of time for which it persists, depends upon the power of the weapon. This photograph was taken 16 milliseconds after the explosion of 'the gadget' during the 'Trinity' test; the hemisphere reaches to about 660ft (200m). *(US Department of Defense)*

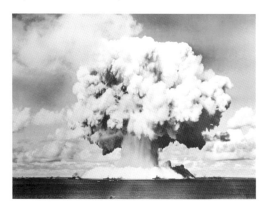

LEFT In July 1946, the USA conducted atmospheric and underwater atomic tests at Bikini Atoll, code-named Operation Crossroads. The tests were assigned the names 'Able' and 'Baker'; the photograph shows one of the 'Baker' explosions, detonated 90ft (27m) underwater. *(US National Archives)*

LEFT 'Baker' test at Bikini Atoll, photographed at the moment of detonation. *(US Department of Defense)*

Crossroads saw the detonation of two weapons, code-named 'Gilda' and 'Helen of Bikini', at Bikini Atoll in the Pacific Ocean, designed to assess the effects of nuclear weapons on shipping. Some 95 captured Japanese vessels were anchored around the atoll and the first test saw 'Gilda' detonated at a height of about 500ft (152m). In the second test, conducted three weeks later, 'Helen' was detonated underwater at a depth of 90ft (27m). A third series of tests was carried out in 1948, under the name Operation Sandstone.

There was no doubt that the genie was now out of the bottle – and there was to be no going back.

Nuclear weapons in Germany

Although the USA was the first nation to successfully produce a nuclear weapon, the outcome of the Second World War would have been very different had the Nazis won the race.

In April 1939, less than six months after Hahn had reported on the discovery of nuclear fission, the Wehrmacht's Heereswaffenamt initiated a top-secret nuclear project to use fission to produce nuclear weapons. In July of that year, the Hungarian physicist Leó Szilárd is said to have warned Albert Einstein that the Germans might be working on producing an atomic bomb. Einstein, who by this time had fled Germany for the USA, signed a letter to President Franklin Roosevelt urging that the USA start work on developing its own atomic bomb.

Hitler's initial interest was in producing a 'dirty bomb', or a 'radiological dispersal device', that could be used to expose Allied civilian populations to radioactive material. It was proposed that a bomb consisting of a shielded casing containing around 1,750lb (800kg) of high explosive surrounded by 440lb (200kg) of radioactive waste could be delivered by either rocket or aircraft and would shower a large area, resulting in multiple deaths from blast, radiation sickness and genetic damage. Dropping such a device on Manhattan, with an estimated 1 million fatalities, might have been sufficient to keep the USA out of the war in Europe.

During 1940, the Germans acquired 'virtually all the uranium in Europe', totalling more than 1,200 tons. Various experiments were planned, but the scientists seemed unable to agree on how to proceed, with rival groups working on carbon-dioxide dry ice, heavy water and electro-graphite as possible moderators for controlling the fission process. It was eventually decided that heavy water would be the most effective moderator, but it is ironic, in the light of what was to follow, that the Wehrmacht concluded that nuclear fission would have little effect in ending the war within the required timescale. In January 1942, the programme was put in the hands of the Reich Research Council, and was divided amongst nine major institutes. Three separate projects were defined: the development of a nuclear reactor (*Uranmaschine*); the production of uranium and the separation of isotopes of uranium-235 and 238; and the production of heavy water, a project that had already been under way in Norway when the Nazis invaded. At the same time, the number of scientists working on the project was reduced. A month later, Werner Heisenberg, one of the lead scientists on the project, presented a lecture to officials of the Council describing energy acquisition from nuclear fission. Heisenberg later told Albert Speer that a bomb could not be built before 1945, and would require significant monetary and manpower resources. After the war it became apparent that he had been deliberately delaying the successful development of a German bomb. Nevertheless, at least two atomic tests were apparently carried out at the secret Nazi underground military facility in the Jonas Valley in Thuringia in 1945, with what Russian observers described as 'a strong radioactive effect'.

When Germany surrendered, a quantity of unprocessed uranium oxide, that was on its way to Japan by submarine, fell into the hands of the Allies.

Nuclear weapons in Japan

In 1938, Japan had purchased a cyclotron particle accelerator from the University of California, Berkeley, and within a year Dr Yoshio Nishina, the leading figure in the nation's atomic programme, had grasped the military potential of nuclear fission. In April 1941, weapons-development programmes were initiated by both the Imperial Army and the Navy, but, by 1942, the latter was convinced that an effective nuclear weapon could not be developed within a reasonable timescale. The naval programme was abandoned until 1943, when it was re-established under Bunsaku Arakatsu at the Imperial University, Kyoto, and described as the F-Go Project.

Meanwhile, the Imperial Army had continued its own research, described as the Ni-Go Project. Germany was asked to collaborate, and some 1,230lb (560kg) of uranium oxide was dispatched to Japan in April 1945 aboard the submarine *U-234*, along with other materials that could aid the Japanese war effort. The U-boat did not reach Japan and surrendered to the US destroyer USS *Sutton* on 16 May 1945. It is said that the fact that the submarine was carrying uranium helped convince President Truman that Japan had a nuclear programme. Since there was no way of confirming progress, the USA resolved to bring the war to a swift conclusion.

The post-war years

At the end of the Second World War, three nations had scientific programmes to develop nuclear weapons. Of these, Japan and Germany were in no position to continue and the USA had already demonstrated that its technology had reached the practical stage. At least for the moment, the USA was the world's only nuclear power. It was an awesome responsibility and, around the world, many expressed their doubts as to how 'the awful secret of the atomic bomb might be kept in the hands of those who are well disposed to their fellow men'. As one commentator pointed out, 'unlike every other instrument of aggressive war, there would seem hardly any chance of inventing an opposing weapon which would effectively counteract its destructiveness'.

And yet, despite the scale of destruction that had been wrought at Hiroshima and Nagasaki, astonishingly, General MacArthur argued that nuclear weapons should be used during the Korean War. This was opposed by both President Truman and his successor, Eisenhower, at least partly on the basis that it would strengthen the Soviet view that the USA was 'bent on initiating general war'. As if this were not bad enough, in 1954 the USA also briefly considered using nuclear weapons to aid

the French during the first Indochina War.

In November 1952, the USA detonated its first thermonuclear device. A test installation for a hydrogen, or fusion, bomb was exploded above Enewetak Atoll in the Pacific, destroying the islet Elugelab and creating a dust cloud 25 miles (40km) high and almost 100 miles (162km) wide. There had been conflicting views from the physicists involved as to whether work on this new weapon should go ahead, and even Robert Oppenheimer, who apparently regretted his involvement in the Manhattan Project, dragged his feet, resulting in the suspension of his security clearance. After much agonising, the project was approved by President Truman at the end of January 1950.

Code-named 'Ivy Mike', the 10.4-megaton warhead used liquid cryogenic deuterium fuel, with a fission device to initiate the fusion reaction, but the physical size of the device made it unsuitable for use as a weapon. Nevertheless, this was the first true hydrogen bomb – or 'H-bomb' – using nuclear fusion

ABOVE 'Castle Bravo' was the first US test of a dry fuel hydrogen bomb; 1 March 1954, Bikini Atoll. *(US Department of Energy)*

LEFT The Mk 17 was the first US-designed thermonuclear device – or hydrogen bomb – to be put into mass production, with a total of 200 devices built. Weighing 21 tons (21.4 tonnes), the Mk 17 had a yield of 10 to 15 megatons. *(US Department of Defense)*

for the explosive yield, rather than fission, and allowing the development of ever-more powerful warheads. In March 1954, during the 'Bravo' trials, US scientists significantly underestimated the yield of a weapon under test. Although the projected yield was 5 megatons, the actual yield was 14.8 megatons, making it the largest weapon to be tested by the USA, and the effects of fallout were measured as far away as 300 miles (500km) from the explosion.

Whilst early nuclear weapons were designed to be dropped from aircraft or delivered by intercontinental ballistic missiles (ICBMs), both the USA and the Soviet Union were keen to develop smaller weapons that could be deployed against ground troops. During Operation Upshot-Knothole, a series of 11 nuclear tests conducted in May 1953, the US Army revealed the first tactical nuclear weapon in the form of the 15-kiloton W19 atomic artillery shell, designed to be fired from the M65 nuclear cannon, colloquially known as 'Atomic Annie'. The shell weighed 805lb (365kg), and was designed to explode around 200ft (60m) above the target.

Tests of new weapons continued, and, during Operation Argus in 1958, a 1.7-kiloton warhead was detonated at an altitude of 125 miles (200km), making it the first atomic weapon to be tested in space. Four years later, in May 1962 at Christmas Island, Operation Dominic 1 was the first, and only, US test of a submarine-launched ballistic missile (SLBM), using a warhead with a 600-kiloton yield.

The Soviet Union

In 1944, Niels Bohr, a Danish physicist, had argued that the Soviet Union should be allowed to participate in the development of nuclear weapons, the better to prepare 'an international control scheme' to prevent the post-war proliferation of such devices. Bohr was unsuccessful, but the Soviet Union, unhappy with its isolation and with the hostile attitude of its former allies, was only too aware of how the balance of power had shifted. Aided by spies placed strategically within the Manhattan Project, Stalin resolved that the Soviet Union should acquire its own bomb.

Yuli Khariton is considered to be the designer of the Soviet bomb, but he was helped considerably by Klaus Fuchs, a German scientist who gave the Soviets stolen plans, including details of 'Fat Man', the weapon that had been used at Nagasaki. Despite difficulties in finding a supply of uranium, the first Soviet test, RDS-1, code-named 'First Lightning', took place on 29 August 1949 with a weapon designated 'Joe-1' by the Americans, that was almost a copy of 'Fat Man'. It would be fair to say that the USA was rattled, and a top-secret report, prepared by the CIA and dated 9 June 1950, concluded that 'the Soviet possession of nuclear weapons has increased the military and subversive capabilities of the Soviet Union and the possibility of war … accordingly, the security of the United States is in increasing jeopardy'. Appearing to support this view, it seems that, had the Soviet-backed attack in Korea in 1950

RIGHT 'Atomic Annie' was the nickname given to the M65 atomic cannon, a 280mm towed artillery piece capable of firing a 15-kiloton nuclear shell across a range of 20 miles (32km). Some 200 examples were constructed, and the cannon was transported by two specially designed Kenworth tractors. *(US Department of Defense)*

been successful, Stalin might have deployed nuclear weapons against Europe.

In 1951, the Soviets conducted their second and third tests. RDS-2, code-named 'Joe-2' by the Americans, was a 38.3-kiloton implosion device using tritium-boosted uranium, whilst RDS-3 ('Joe-3') was an air-dropped 41.2-kiloton weapon of composite construction, using a plutonium core and a shell of uranium. By August 1953, the Soviets had tested their first hydrogen bomb (RDS-6, or 'Joe-4'), in Kazakhstan. It was a 200- to 400-kiloton thermonuclear device using layered fission and fusion fuels (uranium-235 and lithium-6 deuteride), with a fifth of the yield provided by the fusion process. 'Joe-4' created something of a stir as, unlike the USA's first fusion device, it was sufficiently small to be delivered by air.

Two years later, the Soviet leader, Nikita Khrushchev, resolved that he would demonstrate his country's technology to the West by detonating a 100-megaton bomb. Dubbed 'Tsar Bomba', the device was exploded in October 1961 at a height of 11,300ft (3,700m) above the Novaya Zemlya test site. In the event, the yield was just 58 megatons, but the heat radiation produced was sufficient to cause third-degree burns at a distance of 60 miles (100km), and the yield was greater than the total explosives detonated during the Second World War. Too large to be carried inside the Soviet bombers of the period, the device was attached beneath the fuselage and special precautions were taken to prevent damage to the aircraft, with the pilot and co-pilot crew protected, inadequately as it turned out, by 600mm of lead shielding. At the time, this was the largest nuclear device that the world had seen – equivalent to 1 ton of TNT for every head of population in Britain.

Other nations join the 'nuclear club'

Britain was frozen out of the US nuclear programme in 1945, but the British government deemed it essential that the nation had independent nuclear weapons in order to remain a world power. A development programme for an 'independent deterrent' was initiated in January 1947, and by October 1952 Operation Hurricane saw the first bomb,

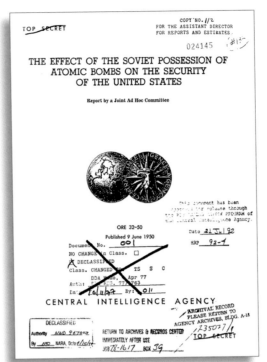

LEFT Secret report, prepared by the CIA in June 1950, which concluded that 'the Soviet possession of nuclear weapons has increased the military and subversive capabilities of the Soviet Union and the possibility of war'. *(US National Archives)*

with a yield of 25 kilotons, tested on the Monte Bello Islands, off the coast of Australia. The first successful British hydrogen bomb, yielding 1.8 megatons, was tested in November 1957 at Christmas Island. In a fit of patriotic fervour the *Daily Express* declared: 'It's our H-bomb', whilst those who were nervous of this new development may have taken comfort in the words of an unnamed Anglican bishop who went on record with his belief that 'our nuclear weapons will be used with wisdom'.

By the following year, the US political climate

BELOW Scientists Frank H. Pavry and George R. Stanbury at Monte Bello, measuring the effects of Britain's first nuclear weapon test during Operation Hurricane; October 1952. *(Warehouse Collection)*

once again permitted co-operation with other nations on nuclear issues, and, in 1960, Britain's independent 'Blue Streak' missile programme was cancelled in favour of joint Anglo-US development. Since that date, despite using home-grown warheads, Britain has relied on the USA for a nuclear delivery system.

In February 1960, France detonated a 70-kiloton atomic weapon, code-named 'Gerboise Bleu', in the Sahara Desert. Further testing was conducted underground until 1967 when a 2.6-megaton thermonuclear weapon was detonated above Fangataufa Atoll, 150 miles (240km) south-west of the Polynesian Gambier Islands. The atoll was so contaminated with fallout that it was uninhabitable for six years, and, as late as 2006, France was still being urged to clean up the resulting radioactive mess. France conducted a further 193 nuclear tests on the Fangataufa and nearby Mururoa Atolls between 1966 and 1996. Of these, 41 were atmospheric and 137 underground; a further 15 were described as 'safety trials'.

China became the fifth nuclear power when it detonated a 25-kiloton uranium device in October 1964 at Lop Nur, with a hydrogen bomb successfully tested in June 1967. The Chinese weapons programme was supported by the Soviet Union until the late 1950s, in exchange for a supply of uranium ore, but work continued independently after tensions emerged between the two nations.

Alongside the USA, Britain, France, the Soviet Union and China, the current roll-call of nuclear nations also includes India, Pakistan and North Korea. India and Pakistan have never agreed to be bound by the 1968 Treaty on the Non-Proliferation of Nuclear Weapons, whilst North Korea acceded from the Treaty in 1985. Israel is also usually included in the list, although it has always refused to confirm that it possesses nuclear weapons despite having been supplied with 20 tons of heavy water which the UK Atomic Energy Authority (UKAEA) had purchased from Norway in 1958. Some 150 to 200 US nuclear weapons have also been stored and deployed in Belgium, Italy, the Netherlands, Turkey and West Germany under the aegis of NATO. Similarly, former-Soviet weapons were deployed to Belarus, Kazakhstan and Ukraine following the break-up of the Soviet Union.

Other nations, including Australia, Canada, Japan and Sweden, are described as either 'virtual nuclear states', or 'para-nuclear states', meaning they have the technical capability to build nuclear weapons but have chosen not to do so. South Africa should also be included in this category since it not only has the capability to produce nuclear weapons, but has actually done so in the past and subsequently destroyed them.

RIGHT Yielding 10.4 megatons, 'Ivy Mike' was the code name of the first US test of a full-scale Teller–Ulam-designed thermonuclear device. The test took place at Enewetak Atoll in the Pacific Ocean in November 1952. *(US Department of Defense)*

East–West arms race

Development of ever-more powerful weapons continued apace during the decades following the end of the Second World War, with huge amounts of money devoted to improving the 'quality' of the weapons and increasing the number of warheads available. By 1953, both sides had developed the infinitely more powerful thermonuclear hydrogen bomb – the 'H-bomb' – which used an initial fission reaction to ignite hydrogen fusion. Described as the Teller–Ulam configuration, from the names of its two chief contributors, Edward Teller and Stanislaw Ulam, the hydrogen bomb is the most efficient design for weapons, with yields above 50 kilotons. Virtually all current nuclear weapons are of the thermonuclear design.

In October 1960, President John F. Kennedy had said that: 'I think the fate not only of our own civilisation, but the fate of the world and the future of the human race, is involved in preventing a nuclear war.' He was right but, despite a popular slogan of the period that decreed 'what this planet needs is more mistletoe and less missile-talk', it didn't seem to bring an end to the madness.

From about 1957, the US Gaither Committee had used the public perception of a 'missile gap' as a political tool to increase military spending, and, within a year, the US defence budget stood at $12 billion. Between 1946 and 1957, the USA amassed more than 5,000 strategic warheads with a combined payload of 5,600 megatons, a figure which the Soviet Union did not reach until the mid-1970s. By 1982, the USA had 11,000 warheads, and, by the end of the decade, was committing 7% of gross domestic product (GDP) to military expenditure. Total US defence spending during the Cold War has been estimated at $8.75 trillion in present-day (2016) terms, half of which was spent on delivery mechanisms.

For a while, the Soviet Union lagged behind but, by 1986, it was reckoned to have 45,000 warheads, of which 20,000 were tactical. By this time, Soviet defence spending had risen to a crippling 15–17% of GDP, and in 1988, Soviet military spending totalled 21 billion roubles, or about $33 billion.

By the mid-1960s, the world nuclear stockpile stood at the equivalent of around 20 tons of TNT per head of population.

Following the 1962 Cuban Missile Crisis, a 'hotline' was established between the Pentagon and the Kremlin, speeding communication between the two sides and reducing the possibility of misunderstandings. The hotline proved invaluable when, in November 1983, Operation Able Archer, a US-led NATO exercise involving 40,000 troops across Europe, was apparently considered to be so realistic the Soviet Union believed that a nuclear strike on its territory was a real possibility. Submarines were deployed under the Arctic ice and more than a dozen bombers put into the air with a nuclear payload.

Like gunslingers in a bad Western movie the two sides continued to glare at one another across the plains of Germany, neither wanting to draw first but each watching the other like a hawk. Considerable sums were spent on clandestine intelligence gathering, a process that actually helped to maintain the status quo, and the world settled into what could be described as an uneasy stalemate punctuated by periods of heightened tension.

Nuclear-weapons-free zones

In an effort to prevent the spread of nuclear weapons, Article VII of the Treaty on the Non-Proliferation of Nuclear Weapons of 1970, grants nation states the right to establish specified nuclear-weapons-free zones (NWFZ). In 1975, the UN General Assembly reaffirmed that right in resolution 3472B. Nations which participate in an NWFZ have committed not to manufacture, acquire, test or possess nuclear weapons.

Although only one such treaty predates the end of the Cold War – the 1967 Treaty of Tlatelolco, which covers Latin America – there are currently nine treaties in place, establishing NWFZs that cover more than half of the earth's land area, including the South Pacific (Treaty of Rarotonga, 1985), South-East Asia (Treaty of Bangkok, 1985), Africa (Treaty of Pelindaba, 1996) and Central Asia (Treaty of Semipalatinsk, 2006), as well as the seabed, the Antarctic and space.

Nuclear-free zones

During the early 1980s, around 200 local authorities in Britain, including the Greater London Council, declared themselves to be 'nuclear free', refusing to participate in civil defence exercises relating to nuclear war and 'forbidding' the movement of nuclear materials through the area controlled by the authority, although, in practice, this was little more than a gesture.

Doomsday clock

In 1947, a group of international researchers, including personnel from the Manhattan Project, developed the Doomsday Clock, a hypothetical timepiece reflecting changes in the level of nuclear peril facing mankind. Describing this clock in the *Bulletin of the Atomic Scientists*, the group, which called itself the Chicago Atomic Scientists, explained that the closer the hands came to midnight, the closer the world was to a nuclear catastrophe. At the time of its inception, the clock was set at seven minutes to midnight, and, since that time, the 'hand' of the clock has moved 18 times, the closest to midnight being two minutes: this came in early 1953 when the USA tested its first hydrogen bomb.

The concept of the clock has subsequently been expanded to include the effects of climate change and, currently (2016) stands at three minutes to midnight.

Fighting a nuclear war

In 1954, Marshal Vasily Sokolovskii, the Soviet Chief of the General Staff, stated unequivocally that 'Soviet Forces are preparing for combat in the atomic age', and it was abundantly clear that the two most powerful nations in the world, together with their respective allies, possessed sufficient firepower to literally wipe out life on earth. Notwithstanding the fact that a 1957 British government White Paper stated that 'there is no defence against nuclear war' – a view that was reinforced by former US President Reagan's declaration that 'nuclear war cannot be won and must not be fought' – it seems that military strategists on both sides were not deterred from planning for such an event.

Many strategists took the view that, although immensely powerful, nuclear weapons were simply another part of the legitimate arsenal to be deployed as and when the situation demanded. The fact that just one bomb might be able to wipe out an entire city was a measure of 'efficiency', not a quantum change in the logistics of conflict. Others, including General Henry 'Hap' Arnold, Commander of

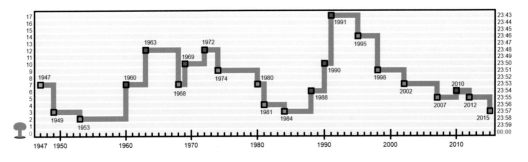

LEFT With a modest 20–30 kiloton yield, the USA's truck-mounted 'Honest John' rocket was the first tactical nuclear weapon to enter service; it was also capable of carrying a non-nuclear payload. *(US Department of Defense)*

US Army Air Forces, took the view that nuclear weapons represented a real revolution in the technology of conflict – as had the use of bows and arrows and the invention of gunpowder. Arnold believed that nuclear weapons had 'lowered the cost of destruction', making it 'cheap and easy'.

Nuclear weapons are frequently described in terms of being a 'deterrent', but what one side regards as a deterrent the other side may well view as a threat, and brinkmanship seemed to be the order of the day. For example, in 1956, speaking from the relative comfort of having a very large nuclear stockpile, US Secretary of State John Foster Dulles explained that 'the ability to get to the verge without getting into the war is the necessary art … if you are scared to go to the brink you are lost'. Edging to the brink of war is one thing – actually being the first to use nuclear weapons is quite another.

In 1980, the US Office of Technology Assessment estimated that a full-scale nuclear exchange would affect somewhere between 3.5 and 25 million in the USA, 16 to 44 million in the Soviet Union and 11 to 37 million elsewhere. The discrepancy between the high and low estimates is huge, but since the Hiroshima and Nagasaki attacks only involved single weapons of relatively low yield, there was little precedent for assessing the effects of larger weapons. The

numbers of casualties would also be affected, for example, by the availability of shelters and protective clothing and equipment, as well as by civil defence procedures dealing with the after-effects of an attack.

Tactical vs strategic weapons

The proponents of nuclear warfare draw a distinction between the tactical, or non-strategic, weapons, which might be used in a limited nuclear exchange, and strategic weapons that are aimed at an entire nation, including military, economic and civilian targets, such as cities and factories. It is the strategic nuclear weapons that strike fear into the heart of the civilian population.

During the Cold War large numbers of the stockpiled weapons were tactical, meaning that they were designed for use on the battlefield, and were of a relatively low yield. For some years, the West considered that superiority in tactical nuclear weapons could offset an inferiority in conventional weapons. However, it became apparent that the Soviets had the capability of deploying either conventional or nuclear weapons at will, and if the decision was taken to use tactical nuclear weapons then multiple strikes would be made on NATO's means of delivering their own nuclear weapons, as well as at headquarters, rear area installations and communication centres. Notes produced for NATO forces in the mid-1970s regarding the deployment of Soviet ground forces suggested that the most likely scenario involved the use of 33 warheads in an initial strike, followed by a further 36 over a period of three days, 18 over the next three days and 13 for the final four days of a ten-day period, giving a total of 100 warheads.

As regards an exchange of strategic nuclear weapons, apart from the devastation that would be caused, this would have long-term effects on life on the planet, causing death, injury and genetic damage. Huge amounts of radioactive fallout would turn large areas into no-go zones, and many scientists believe that the amount of dust and particles released into the atmosphere would lead to a so-called 'nuclear winter', or produce irreversible adverse effects on the environment and the ecological system that could last for decades, or even centuries, after the initial attack.

BELOW The year 1977 saw the first trials of 'Trident', a submarine-launched three-stage ballistic missile with a range exceeding 7,000 miles (11,340km). As of 2016, 'Trident' remains Britain's sole nuclear deterrent. *(US Department of Defense)*

Mutual assured destruction (MAD)

From 1953, believing that it possessed superior and more numerous nuclear firepower, the USA had adopted a strategy that was described as 'massive retaliation'. Had the Soviet Union attacked the USA with nuclear weapons then the response would have been disproportionate, 'dissuading' the other side from such an action, and even as late as 1978, the historian Robert Conquest said that 'there's nothing the Russians can do so long as we keep the level of our arms right'. When the Soviet Union adopted a similar approach, the USA moved to a strategy described as 'flexible response'.

Eventually, the two sides reached near parity in the numbers and power of their weapons, so, in the interests of maintaining the uneasy stalemate, it was essential that neither side gained a technological advantage. However, even though both sides might have equal firepower, should one side decide to launch a comprehensive attack on the other, there remains a window of opportunity for the other side to react before being annihilated. This ability to react, even after having come under attack – a 'second strike' – forms an intrinsic part of a strategy that came to be described as 'mutual assured destruction' – a term which yields the ironically appropriate acronym MAD.

Both the strategy, and the acronym, came from the American scientist John von Neumann who was chairman of the International Ballistic Missile Committee. MAD ensured that any nation that had come under attack would be able to respond with a nuclear retaliation of at least equal force. The 'balance of power', and the prospect of mutual annihilation, were key in preventing 'the other side' (whichever side that was) from taking pre-emptive action: Why would any nation launch a war which neither side had any chance of winning?

There came an alarming wobble in this balance when, in March 1983, President Reagan announced the so-called 'Star Wars' programme. Officially described as the 'strategic defense initiative' (SDI), the system would destroy incoming missiles using lasers or particle beams fired from space. If it worked,

Chapter Two

Nuclear weapons

The science behind both nuclear weapons and nuclear reactors depends on exploiting the colossal amounts of energy stored in the atomic structure of the universe. This energy is released in two ways – either fission, the splitting of a heavy atom, or by fusion, the joining of light atoms. In the case of a nuclear reactor, the energy is released under careful control, but in the case of an atomic weapon it comes as an unimaginable, uncontrolled wave of heat, blast and light that dwarfs the effects of any conventional weapon. As one commentator has described it: 'a million, billion, billion atoms explode in ten seconds'.

OPPOSITE The world's first thermonuclear explosion – or hydrogen bomb – conducted by the USA at Enewetak Proving Grounds; 1 November 1952. *(US Department of Defense)*

All atoms consist of subatomic particles (electrons, protons and neutrons) bound together by nuclear forces, and the diameter of an individual atom is tiny, ranging from about 0.001 to 0.005μm (0.1–0.5nm) depending on the element involved. The positively charged protons, and neutrons, which carry no charge, form the nucleus of the atom, with negatively charged electrons circulating around the nucleus in 'shells'. A neutrally charged atom has an equal number of protons and electrons, and the atomic number of an element indicates the number of protons; for example, hydrogen, which is the lightest atom, has just one proton in its core and has the atomic number 1. Atoms of the same element also exist with different numbers of neutrons, and each of these variations, which are called isotopes, has an atomic mass number, expressed, for example, as uranium-235, which is equal to the number of neutrons and protons in its core. Isotopes are often unstable, and radioactive isotopes, which emit neutrons naturally, possess properties that can be exploited to release nuclear energy.

Early experiments probing the structure of the nucleus involved bombarding radioactive elements – those elements which are inherently unstable as a result of spontaneous nuclear decay – with subatomic particles. Scientists observed that some of these particles were absorbed, some 'bounced' back and others passed through, with neutrons able to penetrate all materials. German chemists Hahn and Strassmann noticed that, whilst bombarding uranium atoms with neutrons, the nucleus

would sometimes fission, at the same time releasing additional neutrons and large amounts of energy. The neutrons that were released had the same effect as those that had been used to bombard the nucleus, with yet more energy and more neutrons being released, leading to what was described as a 'chain reaction'. Some of the neutrons released escape from the fissionable material and, if neutrons are lost at a faster rate than they are produced, the chain reaction will not be self-sustaining. In order to be successful, a nuclear reaction must effectively control the loss of neutrons, and the point at which the neutrons being lost are matched by those being produced is described as the 'critical mass'. A nuclear explosion can only occur if there is sufficient fissionable material to exceed the critical mass.

At first it was believed that the phenomenon could only be created using either uranium-235, which was thought to be extremely rare, or the man-made element plutonium, which had been produced in 1940 by bombarding uranium-238 with deuterons – stable particles consisting of a proton and a neutron. Introducing a neutron into just one uranium-235 nucleus causes it to divide into two lighter and simpler elements, for example barium-141 and krypton-92, described as the fission products. The sum of the atomic weights (ie the total number of protons and neutrons combined) of the fission products is always less than the atomic weight of the original atom because some of the mass is released as free neutrons, yielding millions of electron-volts of energy. The use of sufficient

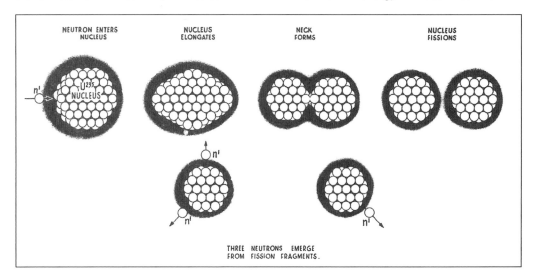

RIGHT Mechanics of fission in uranium-235.
(Warehouse Collection)

quantities of uranium – or plutonium – results in a chain reaction that can be used to create a bomb of colossal power, and even a modest atomic bomb has the explosive power of thousands of tons of conventional explosive.

The first atomic bomb, 'Little Boy', used two slugs of compressed uranium-235 assembled into either end of a 'gun barrel'; an explosive charge at one end fired one of these slugs of fissionable material down the barrel, where it combined with the other to form a critical mass. This was the technology used in the bomb detonated above the city of Hiroshima, and, although it was extremely inefficient, with only an estimated 1.7% of its material fissioning, the weapon yielded a blast equivalent of 15,000 tons of TNT from less than one kilogram (<2.2lb) of uranium. A further 25 'Little Boy' bombs were constructed in 1947, but all had been withdrawn from service by 1951.

The 'gun' technique used for 'Little Boy' was not feasible with plutonium but the material was sufficiently unstable that a chain reaction could be initiated spontaneously without the slugs of fissionable material reaching maximum compression. 'Fat Man' used an 'implosion' technique by surrounding a ball of a little more than one kilogram (>2.2lb) of plutonium with conventional high explosive. When the explosive was detonated, a wave of pressure created a chain reaction in the plutonium, resulting in a blast of destructive energy equal to about 21,000 tons of TNT. Another 120 'Fat Man' bombs were manufactured between 1947 and 1949, but the design was considered obsolete by 1950. These early weapons were primitive by modern standards, producing very modest yields, and further research was directed at reducing the physical size of the bomb, as well as improving the yield and reliability.

A breakthrough occurred with Edward Teller's development of the thermonuclear bomb, a device which increases the potential yield a thousandfold, from kilotons to megatons. Thermonuclear weapons are based on nuclear fusion, a process that creates new elements by fusing light ones together using a mixture of extreme pressure and heat to overcome the natural electrostatic repulsion that exists between the positive charges of atomic nuclei. The process results in a loss of atomic mass

LEFT Billet of highly enriched uranium, in which the uranium-235 content has been increased by isotope separation. Uranium is a silvery-white naturally radioactive heavy metallic element in the actinide series of the periodic table. *(Ames Laboratory; US Department of Energy)*

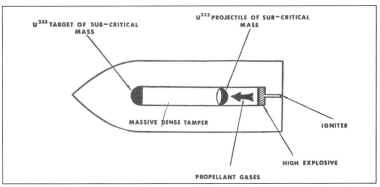

ABOVE Schematic diagram of a gun-type fission weapon; this technology was adopted for 'Little Boy', the bomb dropped on Hiroshima. *(Warehouse Collection)*

BELOW Schematic diagram of implosion-type fission weapon. This technology was adopted for 'Fat Man', the bomb used at Nagasaki. *(Warehouse Collection)*

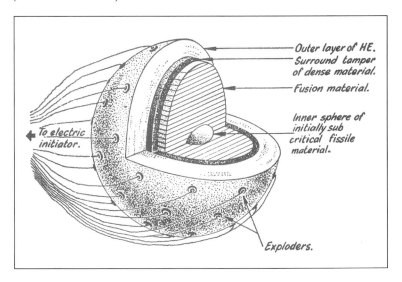

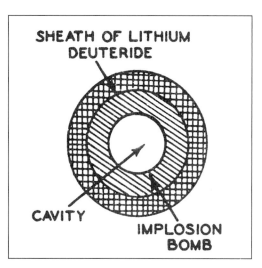

which produces a huge amount of fusion energy. The first tentative thermonuclear bomb, detonated by the Americans in 1951, was effectively a hybrid device, with an atomic primary stage to initiate the secondary, thermonuclear, fusion stage, using isotopes of hydrogen such as deuterium or tritium which were fused to produce helium. The temperatures involved in the process are in the order of 60 million degrees Kelvin, and the amount of energy released depends entirely on the amount of material present in the reaction.

A year later, in 1952, the first full-scale thermonuclear weapon, code-named 'Ivy Mike', with a yield of 10.4 megatons, was detonated on Enewetak Atoll. A large fission bomb was used to trigger the reaction, with liquid deuterium as the fusion fuel. Cryogenic equipment was required to maintain the deuterium in a liquid state, and, although the blast was equivalent to several megatons of TNT, and the heat wave was felt 30 miles (50km) away, this could scarcely be considered a viable weapon. Subsequent devices, initially developed by the Soviet Union, employed a solid sheath of lithium deuteride, and later weapons employed a three-stage process, described as fission-fusion-fission, using a fission bomb to detonate a fusion reaction in lithium-deuteride, sufficient to produce fission in a mass of uranium. This gives a relatively compact weapon producing large quantities of fission products, with the potential for releasing unlimited energy.

Although factually incorrect, this type of weapon is generally described as a 'hydrogen bomb' or 'H-bomb' – a term that has become firmly lodged in the public imagination.

Other types of atomic bomb

In February 1950, the Hungarian-American physicist Leó Szilárd, who had conceived the use of a nuclear chain reaction as a weapon, described a possible 'cobalt bomb' consisting of either a fission or fusion weapon with a sheath of metallic cobalt or a similar material. Its use would result in radiation poisoning that would be sufficient to render affected areas uninhabitable for a century or more. Cobalt weapons were seriously investigated by the USA, but none was ever built or deployed.

The USA, the Soviet Union, France and China have also developed 'neutron bombs' or 'enhanced-radiation weapons'. A low-yield thermonuclear device is constructed in such a way that, rather than being absorbed, the neutrons generated by the fusion reaction are intentionally allowed to escape through a thin casing. A neutron bomb emits about ten times the amount of neutron radiation as a conventional fusion weapon, and is designed specifically to kill by the use of radiation, with a minimal effect on infrastructure through blast or heat.

Development and testing

To ensure that a nuclear device will function correctly, and to assess its likely effect when used, it is necessary to conduct test detonations, and, although a test might be able to demonstrate how a specific weapon performs, it cannot indicate the effect of

ABOVE Operation Upshot-Knothole was a series of nuclear tests carried out in 1953 at the Nevada Test Site. The largest device of the series was 'Ruth', with a yield of 200 kilotons; the smallest was 'Dixie', yielding just 11 kilotons. *(US National Nuclear Security Administration, Nevada Field Office)*

simultaneously detonating multiple weapons over a relatively small area.

Early nuclear tests were made by detonating the device on a tower or suspended from a balloon, or by dropping it from an aircraft. The first underground test was conducted in 1951, and the majority of the tests carried out during the Cold War were underground. This has the advantage that the explosion is contained, and, providing there is no 'venting' to the surface, fallout is minimised.

The warhead, or 'physics package' as it is often termed, is generally tested without the delivery vehicle, and the USA, for example, has conducted fewer than ten tests using an operational missile. Most notable of these was a single test of an ICBM with a nuclear payload during Operation Frigate Bird, when a 'Polaris A2' missile was launched from a submarine across a distance of more than 1,000 miles (1,600km) to a test site on Christmas Island.

RIGHT 'Minuteman' ICBM, capable of carrying up to three nuclear warheads, with a yield of 300–500 kilotons. 'Minuteman' is currently the only ICBM in the US nuclear arsenal.
(US Department of Defense)

Testing also has a propaganda value.
Successful nuclear tests have been used to
signal the scientific and military strength of the
particular nation and, between 1945 and 1963,
the world's nuclear powers conducted almost
600 tests in the atmosphere, with a total yield
of 545 megatons. Concerns began to arise
that the biosphere was being contaminated
by radioactivity: scientific monitoring systems
showed that testing was having a measurable
effect on levels of environmental radioactive
particles and particular concerns were raised
about the levels of radioactive isotopes (or

radionuclides). Levels of strontium-90 in milk
rose considerably following periods of intense
testing during 1961 and 1962, and there were
measurable increases in tritium (hydrogen-3)
and caesium-137, all of which have biological
effects, including damage to DNA and an
increase in various cancers. Discussions about
limiting testing, involving the USA, Britain, the
Soviet Union, Canada and France, had started
back in 1955, but it was not until August 1963
that the Treaty Banning Nuclear Weapon Tests
in the Atmosphere, in Outer Space and Under
Water was signed.

The Treaty did not result in an end to all
testing, and, since 1963, a further 1,352 tests
have been conducted underground with a
total yield of 90 megatons. However, there
was a measurable reduction in environmental
concentrations of specific radionuclides. In
1976, the USA and the Soviet Union agreed
to limit the yield of underground tests to
a maximum of 150 kilotons. Underground
testing continued in the USA until 1992, in
the Soviet Union until 1990 and in Britain to
1991. China and France ended testing in 1996,
but, in January 2016, North Korea, which
had started testing in October 2006, claimed
that it had successfully tested a 'miniaturised'
thermonuclear device.

Nuclear test sites

The tests for the first atomic weapons were
carried out at White Sands Proving Ground near
Alamogordo, New Mexico, but, by the 1950s,
the USA had established a test site in Nye
County, Nevada, with the first test conducted
there on 27 January 1951. Mushroom clouds
rising above the site were visible for hundreds
of miles and radioactive fallout was often carried
by the wind across the state of Utah, leading
to a rise in some forms of cancer, including
leukaemia. Various schemes are currently in
operation to compensate those living downwind
of the Nevada Test Site who may have been
affected; by 2006, the compensation figure paid
to US citizens exposed to nuclear hazards as a
result of the nuclear weapons programme stood
at $1.2 billion.

The USA also tested weapons at a number
of sites in the Pacific, including the Marshall
Islands, from 1946 until about 1960, the first

RIGHT Shell of a typical domestic house constructed at the Nevada Test Site to observe the effects of nuclear weapons on small-scale structures; 1955. *(US National Archives)*

BELOW Crater resulting from a shallow underground 104-kiloton blast carried out during Operation Plowshare at the Yucca Flat Test Site in July 1962; the crater measured 1,280ft (390m) in diameter and was 320ft (97m) deep. The blast was part of a programme designed to investigate the use of nuclear weapons for mining and other civilian purposes. *(US Department of Defense)*

LEFT Multiple craters resulting from nuclear blasts at the Yucca Flat Test Site. *(US Department of Defense)*

LEFT Explosives storage area at the Foulness Test Site of the AWE. The site was in use for the entire period of the Cold War and was used during the development of all of Britain's nuclear weapons, as well as for conducting investigations into the effects of nuclear weapons on buildings. *(Historic England)*

being Bikini Atoll. More than 100 atmospheric tests were carried out until the ratification of the Partial Test-Ban Treaty in 1963 when testing reverted to Nevada. Many of the Pacific islands that were used for testing remain contaminated to this day, and the USA has paid more than $750 million to Marshall Islanders in compensation.

Between 1952 and 1957, a total of 12 major tests, and many minor tests, were carried out by the British at sites in Australia, including Emu Field, at Maralinga in the Great Victoria Desert in South Australia and at the Monte Bello Islands, an archipelago of around 174 small islands off the coast of north-west Australia. Further small-scale testing continued at Emu Field until 1963. Radioactivity from the mainland tests was detected in South Australia, New South Wales, the Northern Territory and Queensland. The sites at Emu Field and at the Monte Bello Islands were both seriously contaminated, with 'significant radiation hazards' remaining even after a 1967 clean-up; at Maralinga, a second attempt to decontaminate the site was made in the year 2000 at a cost of $108 million. More British tests were conducted on Christmas

Island in the Indian Ocean during 1957 and 1958, and at Malden Island in the Pacific. All solo British testing ended in 1958, with joint tests being conducted by Britain and the USA from 1961 at Nellis Air Force Range and the Nevada Test Site.

The health effects of the British tests were no less serious, and, in 2005, a study concluded that sailors who observed the tests at Malden Island suffered adverse effects from exposure to fallout; although subsequently unsuccessful, a class action was filed against the Ministry of Defence (MoD). The Australian government has also paid compensation to former personnel who have suffered health problems, including servicemen who were ordered to watch the tests without any proper protective equipment, and to the Aboriginal Maralinga Tjarutja people.

Soviet weapons tests, both atmospheric and underground, were generally carried out at the Southern Test Site in Semipalatinsk, north-east Kazakhstan, using the Degelen Mountain Test Facility. This was said to be the largest underground nuclear test site in the world, with 181 tunnels, and some 450 tests made here between 1949 and 1989. There was also a

TABLE 1 NUMBERS OF TESTS CONDUCTED BY THE NUCLEAR POWERS

Nation	Number of tests			
	Atmosphere	Underground	Underwater	Total
Tests conducted between 16 July 1945 and 5 August 1963:*				
Britain	21	2	–	23
France	4	4	–	8
Soviet Union	212	–	3	215
USA	222	114	5	341
Tests conducted after 6 August 1963:				
Britain	–	20	–	20
China	23	22	–	45
France	41	134	–	175
India	–	5	–	5
Israel/South Africa**	1	–	–	1
North Korea	–	4	–	4
Pakistan	–	2	–	2
Soviet Union	–	464	–	464
USA	–	598	–	598
Total number of tests conducted between 1945 and 2015, 1,901* **				

* The Partial Test-Ban Treaty, 1963, prohibited testing in the atmosphere and underwater.

** There are suggestions that Israel and South Africa conducted a joint test near Prince Edward Island in 1979; the incident, which is known as the South Atlantic Flash, was picked up by American instruments.

*** Accurate numbers of tests are difficult to verify; other sources suggest that the number of tests conducted since 1945 may be as high as 2,119.

Northern Test Site at Novaya Zemlya, an Arctic Ocean archipelago in north Russia, where a further 224 tests were carried out, including the 1961 test of the 50-megaton 'Tsar Bomba', the most powerful nuclear weapon detonated during the Cold War. Soviet nuclear weapons tests were also conducted in Uzbekistan, Ukraine and Turkmenistan.

The Soviet authorities showed little regard for the effects of testing on the local people or environment, and the consequences of exposure to radiation were rarely made public at the time. For example, the Novaya Zemlya site has been identified as the largest single cause of radioactive contamination in the Arctic, whilst testing at the Semipalatinsk site has been estimated to have impacted the health of some 200,000 local residents. The Semipalatinsk site was closed in 1991, and unguarded fissile material, including quantities of plutonium, was abandoned in tunnels and boreholes. Five years later, a team of Kazakh, Russian and American nuclear scientists and engineers, operating under the strictures of the Nunn–Lugar Cooperative Threat Reduction Program, started a six-year operation to secure these materials, filling boreholes with concrete and sealing the entrances to tunnels.

Other nuclear nations carried out tests in whatever domestic areas were sufficiently remote to maintain secrecy and to protect the population. France, at first, favoured areas of the Sahara Desert in Algeria, which was a French colony until 1962, but, for tests conducted between 1966 and 1970, chose atolls in the French Polynesian Islands. Chinese nuclear tests were generally carried out at Lop Nur, a dried-out salt lake in Mongolia (see Tables 1 and 2, pages 40 and 41).

Effects of nuclear weapons

The destructive effects of nuclear weapons are threefold, consisting of blast, heat and radiation.

A primary difference between a nuclear weapon and a conventional weapon is power. For example, one of the largest pieces of conventional ordnance is the US Air Force's (USAF's) 'mother of all bombs', the GBU-43/B

TABLE 2 NUCLEAR TEST SITES

Nation	Test site locations
Britain	Christmas Island; Emu Field, South Australia; Maralinga, South Australia; Malden Island; Monte Bello Islands
China	Lop Nur, Xinjiang Uygur Province
France	Fangataufa, Tuamotu Archipelago; Mururoa, Tuamotu Archipelago; Reggane, Algeria
India	Pokhran Test Range, Rajasthan
North Korea	Punggye-ri Nuclear Test Site, North Hamgyong Province
Pakistan	Ras Koh Hills, Balochistan Province
Soviet Union	Novaya Zemlya, north Russia; Degelen Mountain Test Facility, Semipalatinsk, Kazakhstan; also various sites in Uzbekistan, Ukraine and Turkmenistan
USA	Alamogordo, New Mexico; Marshall Islands; Nevada Test Site, Nye County, Nevada; Nellis Air Force Range, Nevada

'massive ordnance air blast', equivalent to about 11 tons of TNT. The Soviet Union claimed to have a 'father of all bombs' – the so-called 'aviation thermobaric bomb of increased power' – a fuel-air weapon with a blast equivalent to 44 tons of TNT, said to have a similar effect to a tactical nuclear weapon but without radioactive fallout. However, to put this into perspective, a nuclear explosion of 10 kilotons, a bomb with 40% less power than the 15-kiloton bomb dropped on Hiroshima, is 250 to 1,000 times more powerful than either of these weapons. Larger devices, with yields measured in megatons, are up to a million times more powerful.

As with a conventional weapon, blast crushes and destroys objects in its path, but, unlike a conventional weapon, which can be considered to be like a hammer blow, the shock wave from a nuclear explosion is more of a prolonged 'push': the duration of the blast continuing hundreds of times longer than a conventional high-explosive bomb. In the case of an air burst, elements of the shock wave are also reflected from the ground, which has been heated and compressed, and these elements travel faster than the direct wave, effectively catching it up and reinforcing it. There is also an extended negative or 'suction' phase which has an equal potential to cause damage. The effect of the blast on personnel is considered irrelevant because, at the distances at which it

RIGHT The major
physical effects
associated with
the use of nuclear
weapons are blast
and shock, thermal
radiation and nuclear
radiation, all of
which have the
potential to kill. This
diagram shows the
distribution of energy
in a typical fission
weapon detonated
at an altitude below
100,000ft (30,500m).
(Warehouse Collection)

BLAST
AND
SHOCK
50%

THERMAL
RADIATION
35%

INITIAL
NUCLEAR RADIATION
5%

RESIDUAL
NUCLEAR RADIATION
10%

RIGHT Cartoon-style
diagram produced by
the Australian Army to
warn soldiers of the
effects of rays, heat
and falling objects.
(Warehouse Collection)

A DEADLY TRIPLE THREAT —
RAYS — HEAT — FALLING OBJECTS

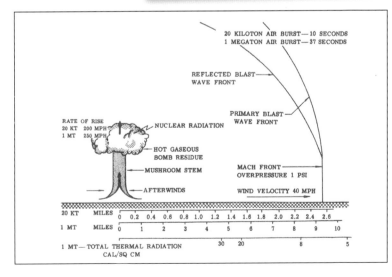

20 KILOTON AIR BURST— 10 SECONDS
1 MEGATON AIR BURST— 37 SECONDS

REFLECTED BLAST
WAVE FRONT

PRIMARY BLAST
WAVE FRONT

RATE OF RISE
20 KT   200 MPH
1 MT   250 MPH

NUCLEAR RADIATION

HOT GASEOUS
BOMB RESIDUE

MUSHROOM STEM

AFTERWINDS

MACH FRONT
OVERPRESSURE 1 PSI

WIND VELOCITY 40 MPH

20 KT   MILES   0   0.2 0.4 0.6 0.8 1.0 1.2 1.4 1.6 1.8 2.0 2.2 2.4 2.6

1 MT   MILES   0   1   2   3   4   5   6   7   8   9   10

1 MT — TOTAL THERMAL RADIATION
CAL/SQ CM   30   20   8   5

would kill, the effects of the subsequent heat
and radiation are much greater.

The blast is followed by a massive wave of
intense light and heat, and a release of radiation.
The light and heat will actually arrive at the
target before the slower-moving blast wave,
whilst the radioactive products resulting from the
disintegration of the bomb itself arrive later.

Directly beneath the explosion is the area
described as 'ground zero'. Here, at the
moment of the explosion, an intense ball of fire
rises up on a column of hot gas thousands of
feet into the air, carrying vaporised rock, dust,
smoke and debris, whilst strong after-winds also
carry debris into the air. The column billows out
at the top into the distinctive mushroom shape.
Most of the heat is produced within the first
second of the explosion, and the temperature
is dependent on the type of weapon and not
its yield. An Australian Army manual written in
1955 to describe the effects of atomic weapons
stated that, 0.1 milliseconds after detonation,
the ball of fire consists of 'an isothermal sphere
with a radius of 50ft (15.25m) at a temperature
of 300,000°K'; later estimates for thermonuclear
weapons put the temperature at 10,000,000°K.
At close range, the wave of heat and light,
which includes infrared, ultraviolet light, is
lethal, but even at some distance is capable of
causing blindness and severe burns, as well as
starting a firestorm.

The third effect of a nuclear weapon consists
of radiation produced during the fission process
in the form of penetrating gamma rays and
neutrons, both of which are lethal. Alpha and
beta particles are also produced as a result
of the decay of the products of fission, and
neutron-induced activity in the soil and in other
materials. The initial period of radiation is brief,
but transitions into a much longer period, during
which there is considerable residual radiation.
Some of the radiation products created exhibit
a half-life – the time it takes for half the nuclei

LEFT Diagram showing the chronological
development of the effects of air-burst nuclear
weapons, firstly, a 20-kiloton weapon, 10
seconds after detonation, and, secondly, from a
1-megaton weapon, 37 seconds after detonation.
(Warehouse Collection)

in a radioactive substance to disintegrate spontaneously – that can range from days to millennia. For example, caesium-137, which is a major source of radiation in nuclear fallout, has a half-life of 30 years, whilst the half-life of uranium-235 is more than 700 million years and that of uranium-238 is 4.5 billion years.

And, sadly, the notion that cockroaches will be the only creatures to survive a nuclear war is a myth. Whilst a dose of 1,000 rads – the standard centimetre–gram–second (CGS) measurement for absorbed radiation – is sufficient to kill a human being after just ten minutes, even a cockroach cannot survive beyond 20,000 rads. Some insects can survive higher rates of exposure, but the bacteria *Deinococcus radiodurans*, which has been dubbed 'Conan the Bacterium', can resist 1.5 million rads, and in a genetically modified form has been used to digest heavy metal and solvent residues during clean-up operations on highly radioactive sites.

Electro-magnetic pulse

Nuclear explosions, particularly those occurring in the upper atmosphere, also create an electro-magnetic pulse (EMP) as the wave of gamma rays hit the upper atmosphere. This surge of electro-magnetic radiation is reflected back at the earth at the speed of light across a wide area, travelling along power lines, cables, metal surfaces, antennas and so on. A power line that is several miles long will absorb tens of thousands of amps, which will disrupt, damage or destroy sensitive electrical and electronic equipment by inducing surges of current and voltage. The pulse can affect communications systems, computing equipment and electronics used, for example, in aircraft and motor vehicles. The effect is not consistent, but a deliberate EMP attack has the capacity to totally destroy a nation's military and civilian electrical

and technological infrastructure, effectively turning the clock back to the 19th century.

It is possible to make electronic components and systems resistant to this damage, and to the possibility of malfunction, by a process described as 'radiation hardening'.

US nuclear weapons

The nuclear weapons deployed against Hiroshima and Nagasaki were physically large – 'Little Boy', for example, was 10ft (3m) long and weighed 9,700lb (4,400kg) – and were simply dropped from a modified Boeing B-29 Superfortress. For tactical weapons this remained the optimum situation for some years. Smaller weapons were subsequently developed, capable of being delivered by short- and medium-range rockets or fired from cannons, but the introduction of ICBMs during the 1950s was considered something of a turning point. ICBMs

offered a more reliable and less vulnerable means of delivery across long distances, but, from the beginning of the 1960s, started to be replaced by submarine-launched weapons with a range of more than 3,000 miles (5,000km).

To date, the USA has produced over 100 different types of nuclear warhead and dozens of delivery vehicles. Early weapons were identified using 'mark' numbers, with the series running from Mk 4 to Mk 101, with 'Little Boy', the abandoned 'Thin Man' and 'Fat Man' being considered Mks 1 to 3. Around 1960, this practice was discontinued, with later weapons identified by an alphanumeric 'W' or 'B' code: the 'W' prefix, for example W78, indicates that the specific weapon is a warhead, whilst 'B' identifies a bomb designed to be delivered by aircraft. Individual US nuclear weapons are described, according to their method of delivery, in Chapters Four to Six.

Although NATO currently includes three nuclear states – the USA, Britain and France – the USA continues to provide the majority of NATO's 'nuclear umbrella'. For logistical reasons, a large proportion of the US European nuclear stockpile was based in Britain during the Cold War, and in a pamphlet published at the beginning of the 1980s, the Campaign for Nuclear Disarmament (CND) claimed that the USA had more than 100 'military facilities' in Britain, including 17 weapons dumps. In 1981, the announcement that 160 US cruise missiles would be based at Greenham Common and Molesworth saw the beginnings of a protest that would continue for almost 20 years, and, even as late as 2005, the *Guardian* was claiming that there were still over 100 American nuclear warheads in store at RAF Lakenheath.

Independent British nuclear deterrent

Although Britain had developed an 'independent nuclear deterrent', US bombs and missiles were stationed in Britain, and, for that matter, elsewhere across the world, throughout the Cold War. Britain also provided bases for US bombers and early warning equipment, and these weapons and facilities helped to provide a nuclear shield for Britain and Europe. Unfortunately, they also ensured Britain was a target for the Soviet Union.

However, the notion of Britain's 'independent deterrent' is, at least partly, an illusion. In 1955, Churchill spoke of Britain possessing 'the most up-to-date nuclear weapons, and the means of delivering them', but, in truth, Britain has tended to rely on US technology. Moreover, Britain's Cold War posture, including the choice of targets, was almost entirely dependent on the USA, with operational control of the V-Bomber force, and the subsequent 'Polaris' and 'Trident' weapons, assigned to the Supreme Allied Commander Atlantic (SACLANT).

The British nuclear bomb
Research into the development of nuclear weapons in Britain started in 1940 when two scientists working at the University of

BELOW Developed during the late 1950s, 'Atlas' was one of the first ground-launched ICBMs, and was capable of delivering a 1.44-megaton W49 warhead across 9,000 miles (14,500km). *(US Department of Defense)*

Birmingham, Otto Frisch and Rudolf Peierls, suggested that the fission of uranium-235 could provide the basis for a weapon. A year later, a report on the military application of uranium fission was produced under the direction of Sir Henry Tizard. A copy was sent to the Uranium Committee in the USA, ultimately leading to the creation of the Manhattan Project and the subsequent bombing of Hiroshima and Nagasaki in 1945. British scientists Otto Frisch, Rudolf Peierls, Geoffrey Taylor and William Penney were amongst those transferred to the USA to support the project.

In 1946, the US Atomic Energy Act – often described as the McMahon Act – outlawed co-operation in research and development on nuclear weapons between the USA and other nations. With no alternative course available if Britain was also to have nuclear weapons, in 1947 Prime Minister Clement Attlee authorised the development of an independent British nuclear weapons programme. The work was led by Dr William Penney, the then Chief Superintendent of Research and Armaments, with Lord Portal appointed as Controller of Production, Atomic Energy. In June 1947, Penney began putting his research and development team together to design a plutonium bomb. The project was initially based at Woolwich Arsenal in south-east London, with contributions coming from the nearby Armaments Research and Development Establishment at Fort Halstead in Kent. Construction work on reactors for the production of plutonium started in September 1947 at Sellafield in Cumbria, with the first reactor completed by October 1950; the plutonium plant came on line in April 1952. The military research programme was moved from Woolwich to a former RAF airfield at Aldermaston in Berkshire in 1950, and two years later the site became known as the Atomic Weapons Research Establishment (AWRE), operating under the auspices of the Ministry of Supply (MoS). In 1954, all British atomic research was transferred to the UKAEA, and a year later, the decision was taken to develop a British thermonuclear device.

There were also commercial aspects to the project, and work was carried out at Harwell in Oxfordshire and Risley in Lancashire to

exploit nuclear fission for energy production. Britain's first nuclear reactor, known as Britain Experimental Pile Zero, was commissioned at Risley in July 1948.

The first weapon, a plutonium implosion device with a yield of 25 kilotons, code-named 'Hurricane', was ready for testing by October 1952. Clearly there was nowhere in Britain where tests could be conducted, and the device was detonated inside the hold of the obsolete frigate HMS *Plym*, anchored offshore at Trimouille Island in the Monte Bello Islands group. The ship was almost completely vaporised and the weapon created a large crater on the seabed. Before the test had been carried out, Penney had suggested that, although timing was 'tight', it might be possible for a 'completely-proven weapon to be in service by mid-1954'.

By November 1953, 'Hurricane' had evolved into 'Blue Danube', sometimes described as 'Smallboy' or 'atom bomb Mk 1'. 'Blue Danube' was a 10- to 12-kiloton air-dropped free-fall bomb based on the American Mk 4. It was developed for production into a composite plutonium/uranium weapon capable of being carried in the bomb-bays of Britain's V-Bombers. A series of four tests were conducted at Emu Field, South Australia, under the code name Operation Totem, and plans were drawn up to manufacture a stockpile of

ABOVE The first nuclear weapon to be produced by Britain in quantity was code-named 'Blue Danube', a 10- to 12-kiloton composite plutonium/uranium air-dropped free-fall bomb based on the American Mk 4. A total of about 60 examples were constructed. *(RAF Museum, Crown Copyright)*

LEFT Designed to be delivered by V-Bomber, 'Blue Danube' was a physically large weapon. It measured 24ft (7.32m) in length, and had a diameter of 60in (1,524mm); the complete weapon weighed 10,000lb (4,636kg). *(Warehouse Collection)*

BELOW Dating from 1955, 'Orange Herald' was a fission-fusion weapon with a yield of 720 kilotons, designed to be mounted on a missile. *(Warehouse Collection)*

BELOW In 1958, 'Blue Danube' was replaced by the more compact 'Red Beard'; the latter had a tritium-boosted fissile core, with a yield of 15–25 kilotons. The smaller size of this weapon allowed up to four to be carried in a V-Bomber. This example was photographed at the test compound of the **AWE.** *(RAF Museum, Crown Copyright)*

FAR LEFT Operation Grapple was a series of nine thermonuclear atmospheric tests carried out by the British between 1956 and 1958 at Malden and Christmas Islands in the Central Pacific. *(Ministry of Defence)*

LEFT The largest weapon of the 'Grapple' series was code-named 'Z3 Halliard 1', with a yield of 800 kilotons. The final weapon of the series, code-named 'Z4 Burgee 2', was used in the last atmospheric nuclear test carried out by Britain. *(Ministry of Defence)*

up to 800 of these weapons, although, in fact, less than 60 were actually constructed. The first example was delivered to RAF Wittering in November 1953, despite no aircraft being available until the following year. 'Blue Danube' was replaced by the more compact 'Red Beard' in 1958, using a tritium-boosted fissile core, with a yield of 15 to 25 kilotons.

Operation Mosaic, which was also conducted at Trimouille Island, during May and June 1956, was intended to further the development of a British thermonuclear device. By January 1957, this led to the development of two alternative devices: 'Green Granite', intended to be delivered by missile, and 'Orange Herald'. There were large and small versions of both weapons, but, at the last minute, the large version of 'Green Granite' was replaced by a third device code-named 'Purple Granite'. During November 1957, a series of tests described as Operation Grapple showed that the performance was below expectations and it wasn't until later in the year that the yields were increased to around 1 to 3 megatons.

A number of test series were also carried out involving nuclear material used in conjunction with a conventional explosion in order to study, for example, the dispersal of radiation.

Following the successful 'Grapple' tests, the first deployable British thermonuclear weapon appeared in the form of 'Yellow Sun' Mk 1, using a tamper-boosted 'layer cake' warhead

code-named 'Green Bamboo', but this was subsequently replaced by the 'Green Grass' pure-fission warhead, and then by the 'Red Snow' warhead, similar to the American W28. In this latter form, the weapon was described as 'Yellow Sun' Mk 2, and is often considered to be the definitive British thermonuclear weapon. The first of around 150 examples of 'Yellow Sun' Mk 2 entered service in 1961, displacing the existing 'Blue Danube'. The 'Green Grass' warhead was also installed in a

BELOW Following the successful 'Grapple' tests, the first deployable British thermonuclear weapon appeared in the form of 'Yellow Sun' Mk 1, seen here during loading trials with a Vulcan bomber at Farnborough; 1962. *(RAF Museum, Crown Copyright)*

TABLE 3 BRITISH NUCLEAR BOMBS, MISSILES AND WARHEADS IN SERVICE 1953–80

Date in service	Designation	Description	Range (where applicable)	Yield
Bombs and missiles				
1953	'Blue Danube' Mk 1, Mk 2	Free-fall bomb; composite plutonium/uranium fission warhead	–	10–12 kilotons
1958	'Violet Club'	Free-fall bomb; 'Green Grass' uranium fission warhead	–	500 kilotons
1958	'Yellow Sun' Mk 1	Free-fall bomb; 'Green Bamboo' or 'Green Grass' uranium fission warhead	–	400 kilotons
1960	'Red Beard'	Free-fall bomb; tritium-boosted plutonium/uranium fission warhead	–	15–25 kilotons
1961	'Yellow Sun' Mk 2	Free-fall bomb; 'Red Snow' thermonuclear fusion warhead	–	1.1 megatons
1962	'Blue Steel'	Air-to-surface strategic stand-off missile; 'Red Snow' thermonuclear fusion warhead	120 miles (200km)	1.1 megatons
1966	WE177B	Free-fall bomb; thermonuclear fusion warhead	–	450 kilotons
1969	'Ikara'	Ship-launched nuclear depth charge; WE177A thermonuclear fusion warhead	12 miles (19km)	0.5 kilotons
1969	WE177A	Free-fall bomb; thermonuclear fusion warhead	–	0.5–10 kilotons
1980	WE177C	Free-fall bomb; thermonuclear fusion warhead	–	200 kilotons
Warheads				
1954	'Green Bamboo'	Fission-fusion warhead	–	1 megaton
1954	'Green Granite'	Fission-fusion warhead	–	1 megaton
1955	'Orange Herald'	Fission-fusion warhead	–	720 kilotons
1957	'Green Grass'	Fission warhead	–	400 kilotons
1958	'Red Snow'	Thermonuclear fusion warhead		1.1 megatons
1970	ET317	Thermonuclear fission-fusion-fission warhead for British 'Polaris' ballistic missiles	–	200 kilotons
1982	'Chevaline'	Thermonuclear fission-fusion-fission multiple warhead for British 'Polaris' ballistic missiles	–	200 kilotons

modified 'Blue Danube' casing, but the resulting weapon, known as 'Violet Club', was fragile and unreliable and only a handful were produced.

The last all-British nuclear warhead and delivery vehicle was the Avro 'Blue Steel', an air-to-surface strategic missile carrying a 1.1-megaton 'Red Snow' thermonuclear warhead. Described as a 'stand-off' weapon, meaning that it could be launched against a target whilst the launch vehicle remained outside the range of enemy surface-to-air missiles, 'Blue Steel' was designed to be carried by a Vulcan or Victor bomber. Development started in 1956, with the first of around 50 examples entering service in December 1962; the last was withdrawn at the end of 1970. A long-range version, designated 'Blue Steel II', was briefly considered, but was cancelled in favour of the American 'Skybolt' system.

By 1961, British research into independent delivery systems had ended and all further developments were made in co-operation with the USA.

The last tactical nuclear warhead used by the British armed forces, and the last nuclear weapon to serve with the RAF, was WE177, a warhead suitable for delivery by air as either a bomb or a helicopter-launched depth charge. The design of WE177 had been initiated in 1960 under the original designation RE179, when Britain had agreed it would purchase the American 'Skybolt' system. The warhead was manufactured in three versions from 1966: WE177A was a boosted-fission device with a variable yield of between 0.5 and 10 kilotons intended to replace 'Red Beard', whilst WE177B and WE177C were thermonuclear fusion devices with yields of 450 and 200 kilotons respectively. A total of 319 examples were constructed: 107 of the WE177A variant, 53 of the WE177B and 159 of the WE177C; all had been withdrawn by 1998.

As well as evolving into WE177, RE179 was also developed into the 200-kiloton ET317 warhead, a hybrid fission-fusion-fission version of the US W59 warhead, designed and manufactured by the Atomic Weapons Establishment (AWE) in collaboration with the Americans. This was used to equip British 'Polaris' missiles, with subsequent improvements to the warhead made under the code name 'Chevaline'. When 'Trident 2' entered service, ET317 was replaced by a British-produced warhead based on the American W76 with a selective yield of 0.3, 5–10 or 100 kilotons (see Table 3, page 48).

Abandoned projects

Many British development projects were abandoned before entering production. For example, 'Blue Slug', a ship-to-ship guided weapon, was discontinued in 1956, as was 'Green Cheese', an air-to-surface anti-ship missile. 'Blue Peacock', also known as 'Brown Bunny', 'Blue Bunny' and 'Big Bertha', was a 10-kiloton atomic landmine, but was cancelled in 1957, as was the 'Violet Mist' landmine. 'Blue Rosette', a free-fall bomb for the Avro 730 bomber, was also discarded in 1957. 'Pixie', a lightweight 1-kiloton plutonium device that used cobalt metal pellets as a diagnostic tool for measuring yield, was tested in 1957, but was subsequently abandoned as being too expensive. 'Indigo Hammer', a 6-kiloton plutonium implosion device intended for the 'Bloodhound' air-defence missile, was axed in 1958. The requirement for a nuclear warhead for 'Sea Slug', a naval surface-to-air guided weapon, was cancelled in 1962. And finally, 'Yellow Anvil' was a proposed 1-kiloton nuclear artillery shell, scrapped in 1958.

Cancelled British missile projects of the period included 'Blue Streak', a medium-range ballistic

BELOW 'Blue Peacock' was a British atomic landmine with a yield of 10 kilotons, designed to be detonated remotely. Also known as 'Brown Bunny', 'Blue Bunny' and 'Big Bertha', it was cancelled in 1957 without going into production.
(Warehouse Collection)

missile and satellite launch vehicle, which was cancelled in 1960 before reaching production, and 'Blue Water', a battlefield, or tactical, nuclear weapon of the late 1950s designed to be used against ground troops. 'Blue Water' was intended to replace the American 'Corporal' system, but was abandoned in 1962.

Anglo-US development

In 1958, a new US Atomic Energy Act overturned the McMahon Act of 1946 which had outlawed US co-operation on nuclear research with other nations. The new act was proposed by Lewis Strauss, Chairman of the Atomic Energy Commission, and included a clause that allowed the President to share information and research on nuclear weapons and fissile material with allies that were making a 'substantial and material contribution to national defense and security' – one such nation was Britain.

Collaboration between the two nations, under a scheme designated Project E, provided Britain with a large number of nuclear weapons, including Mk 5, 7, 28, 43 and 57 free-fall bombs, missiles, naval depth charges, and 8in and 155mm nuclear artillery rounds. The hardware, which started to become available from October 1958, remained under the guardianship of the USA but would have been released for use by British forces had the need arisen, and some US weapons remained available to British forces until the end of the Cold War. As regards delivery vehicles, the lack of success of the 'Blue Steel' and 'Blue Streak' missiles led to the decision that Britain would adopt the US 'Skybolt' missile as a mount for the AWE-designed ET317 warheads. When 'Skybolt' was cancelled in 1962, a deal was thrashed out that allowed Britain to deploy American 'Polaris', and then 'Trident' missiles, albeit with British warheads.

Initially, the missiles were carried in four *Resolution*-class nuclear submarines, each vessel having 16 missiles, armed with a British-built hybrid fission-fusion-fission version of the W59 1-megaton thermonuclear warhead, designated ET317. Each missile could deliver three thermonuclear warheads to a single target. In 1994, the *Resolution*-class submarines were replaced by the new *Vanguard* class, and, at the same time, 'Polaris' missiles were superseded by 'Trident'. Since 1998, 'Trident' has been the only operational nuclear weapons system in British service, with warheads, similar to the American W76, constructed by AWE at Aldermaston.

Political debate continues regarding the possible replacement of 'Trident'.

LEFT In 1994, 'Polaris' was replaced in British service by the American 'Trident', with a British-built warhead similar to the W76. 'Trident' was also designed to be launched from a submarine, in this case the USS *Henry M. Jackson*. *(Bob Duff; US Department of Defense)*

LEFT As of 2016 the 'Trident D5' is Britain's only nuclear deterrent. The *Vanguard*-class submarines from which 'Trident' is launched are scheduled for replacement before 2030, at a likely cost of £15–20 billion, including refurbishment of the warheads. *(Lockheed Martin)*

LEFT Aerial view of the massive Pantex site located north-east of Amarillo, Texas. The 16,000-acre (6,500-hectare) Pantex plant is the only nuclear weapons assembly and disassembly facility in the USA, currently employing around 3,600 people. *(US Department of Defense)*

CENTRE The last example of the 9-megaton Mk 53 (later B53) bomb photographed at Pantex, prior to dismantling. The Mk 53 went into production in 1962 with a total of 340 constructed; it was withdrawn in 1997, and the last one was disassembled on 25 October 2011. *(US National Nuclear Security Administration)*

Nuclear weapons manufacture

The first American nuclear weapons were produced at the Los Alamos National Laboratory in a modest production facility code-named 'Site S'; further production facilities were established at two sites in California, the Naval Ordnance Test Station at China Lake and the Salt Wells Pilot Plant. When production started in earnest, components for 'Fat Man' Mk 3 were produced at the Iowa Army Ordnance Plant, at Rock Island Arsenal, and at Salt Wells, the latter site having been the subject of huge expenditure and expansion. The Salt Wells plant closed in 1954, but the National Laboratory at Los Alamos remains active in research and development, along with other organisations. The production of plutonium-239 and uranium-235 currently takes place at the Y-12 National Security Complex in Tennessee, as well as in Ohio and Washington. Tritium, which is essential to the manufacture of boosted-fission weapons, was processed at the Savannah River Site, near Aiken, South

LEFT Based at Aldermaston, Berkshire, the AWE has been home to Britain's atomic weapons programme since 1950. AWE is responsible for maintaining the warheads for 'Trident', designing new atomic weapons, and dismantling and decommissioning redundant warheads. *(Historic England)*

Chapter Three

Early warning systems

⊏━●━━━━━━━━━━━━━━━━⊐

Throughout the Cold War, NATO and the Warsaw Pact faced each other across the Iron Curtain, each side presuming that the other was only deterred from launching a pre-emptive strike by the prospect of an instant, and deadly, 'second-strike' retaliation. However, in order to be in a position to launch a 'second strike', it is necessary to know exactly, and in real time, what your enemy is up to.

OPPOSITE Work on what was eventually 1,563 ROC underground monitoring posts began in May 1956. The photograph shows the ventilation shafts and equipment post for a typical monitoring post at Lutterworth. *(Nick Catford)*

From 1946 to the mid-1950s, NATO commanders believed that the most likely Cold War scenario involved Soviet bomber aircraft making pre-emptive strikes against cities or manufacturing centres, almost certainly in Europe. Any such strikes would, necessarily, be cataclysmic, and it was essential to maintain vigilance over the actions of the other side by whatever means were available, thus allowing a retaliatory strike to be launched whilst the enemy's missiles were still in the air. An essential component of this vigilance was the electronic early warning system – a chain of passive defence measures, together with the command and control centres that interpreted data received and made decisions regarding retaliation.

Most early warning systems use ground-based radar, but, ultimately, the equipment is also carried in airborne warning and control system (AWACS) aircraft; satellites are also used, in conjunction with infrared detection.

US early warning systems

During the Second World War, the USA established a series of perimeter radar installations along the Atlantic and Pacific coasts of Canada and Alaska to provide early warning of any Japanese air attack. Most were abandoned at the end of the war, but, in response to increasing East–West tension, five stations were refurbished to detect Soviet aircraft entering US airspace under what was described as the 'radar fence'. Further stations

were upgraded as part of a programme that was eventually designated Operation Lashup.

A total of 43 stations went into operation in 1950 under the control of Air Defense Command (ADCOM), and, ultimately, 129 radar stations provided coverage across the continental USA. These were supplemented by four concentric arcs of early warning stations described as: the Alaska Radars; the Pinetree Line, the second phase of which was constructed and financed by the Canadian government; the Mid-Canada Line; and the Distant Early Warning Line (DEW), constructed along the edge of Canada's polar ice cap. Although the threat of attack from aircraft had diminished considerably by the end of the 1960s, the DEW was modernised during the 1980s, with a further 15 long-range radar facilities at existing stations. Redesignated the North Warning System, it became operational in 1994, two or three years after the end of the Cold War.

ADCOM became Aerospace Defense Command in 1968 and was broken up in 1979. The atmospheric defence resources, including interceptors, warning radars, and associated bases and personnel, were transferred to Air Defense, Tactical Air Command (ADTAC), whilst the missile warning and space surveillance assets were transferred to Strategic Air Command, along with control of the USA's land-based bomber aircraft and land-based ballistic missile strategic nuclear arsenal, an arrangement that ended in 1992. ADTAC was

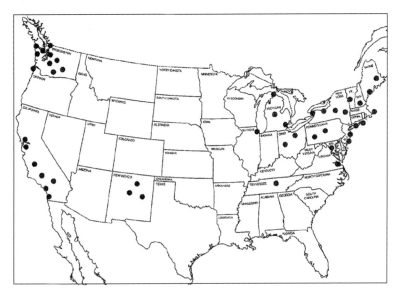

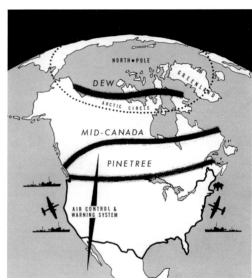

ABOVE **DEW Line station at Point Lay, Alaska.**
(US Department of Defense)

RIGHT In 1958, the USA started construction of the advanced BMEWS, which extended as far as Alaska and Greenland. The photograph shows Clear Air Force Station, Alaska. *(US Army Corps of Engineers)*

dismantled in December 1985 and the assets passed to the Air National Guard.

As the threat of aircraft attack became less likely, the possibility of missile attack grew, and, in 1958, RCA (Radio Corporation of America) was contracted to construct an advanced ballistic missile early warning system (BMEWS) extending as far as Alaska and Greenland. Designated 474L – sometimes known as 'Big L' – BMEWS comprised a network of 12 stations with radar, computer and communications equipment designed to detect a mass ballistic missile attack directed at the northern approaches of the USA. Construction was completed in 1961, and the system went live during 1962/63, providing a 15- to 25-minute warning for the US military. The scanners were said to have a range of 5,000 miles (8,000km), and the BMEWS included the iconic domes at the radar station at RAF Fylingdales in North Yorkshire. It was claimed in 1960 that these domes would give the USA an extra 15 minutes' warning – something that was unlikely to benefit Britain!

LEFT Tracker buildings and the distinctive radomes at RAF Fylingdales, North Yorkshire. Constructed in 1962, Fylingdales formed a vital part of the BMEWS. *(Historic England)*

By 1960, the USA had also established 'Midas', a missile defence alarm system relying on a series of satellites that used infrared detection to provide early warning of the launch of Soviet ICBMs; 12 satellites were planned, but, in the end, just 9 were deployed. 'Midas' was intended to work in conjunction with the ground-based BMEWS, and, although not generally considered to be a success, the 'Midas' programme pioneered the technology that led to the development of the Defense Support Program (DSP) from 1970, and the space-based infrared system (SBIRS), the latter including a NATO communications site at RAF Menwith Hill in Yorkshire.

British early warning systems

During the first decade of the Cold War, Britain's early warning system consisted of 36 radar stations situated down the eastern and southern edge of the country. Originally part of the 'Chain Home' system, the equipment had been installed from about 1936 to detect incoming aircraft, and elements of 'Chain Home' continued in use until the mid-1950s. By 1948, the radar stations had been supplemented by 1,420 observation and monitoring posts from which men of the Royal Observer Corps (ROC), under control of RAF Fighter Command, maintained a vigil on the skies across Britain and Northern Ireland. Each ROC post housed three personnel, many of them civil defence volunteers, equipped with simple instruments

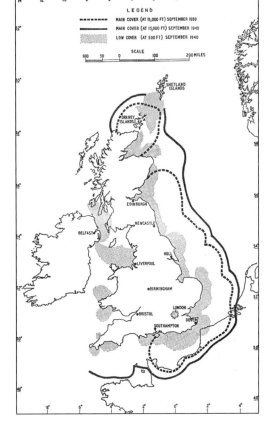

LEGEND

MAIN COVER (AT 15,000 FT) SEPTEMBER 1939
MAIN COVER (AT 15,000 FT) SEPTEMBER 1940
LOW COVER (AT 500 FT) SEPTEMBER 1940

SCALE
100   50   0   100   200 MILES

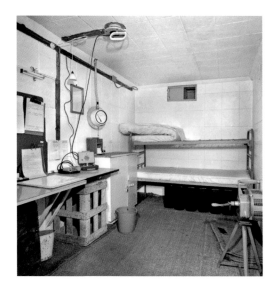

ABOVE Interior view of a restored ROC monitoring post at Knockholt, Kent. The large dial on the left-hand wall is the BPI. *(Nick Catford)*

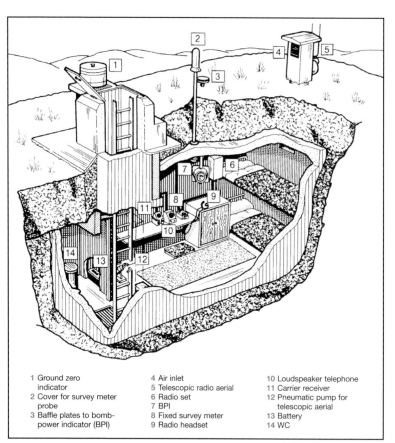

1 Ground zero indicator
2 Cover for survey meter probe
3 Baffle plates to bomb-power indicator (BPI)
4 Air inlet
5 Telescopic radio aerial
6 Radio set
7 BPI
8 Fixed survey meter
9 Radio headset
10 Loudspeaker telephone
11 Carrier receiver
12 Pneumatic pump for telescopic aerial
13 Battery
14 WC

that could gauge the location and power of a nuclear blast. Incredibly, although many of the posts have now been demolished, elements of the system remained in use until 1991/92.

With the first Soviet test of a nuclear weapon, combined with the increasing speed of enemy bombers, it was clear that these somewhat makeshift arrangements could not continue and, in the late 1940s, the government embarked on a modernisation programme for Britain's early warning radar system under the name 'Rotor'. In 1949, the Cherry Report proposed that the number of 'Chain Home' stations be reduced to 66 and that the electronics be upgraded and protected against enemy attack. At the same time, RAF Fighter Command was rearranged into six operational sectors, and the system was integrated with the Army's anti-aircraft defences. In August 1952, the 'Rotor' programme was assigned 'super priority' status, putting it on a par with the development of the nuclear weapons themselves.

The programme was carried out in three phases – 'Rotor 1', 'Rotor 2' and 'Rotor 3' – with the majority of the work executed by the Marconi Wireless and Telegraph Company. 'Rotor 1' consisted of 34 'Chain Home' stations, 8 early warning stations, 11 underground control interception stations and 14 semi-submerged above-ground interception stations. From 1954,

ABOVE Cutaway view of a typical ROC monitoring post. *(Warehouse Collection)*

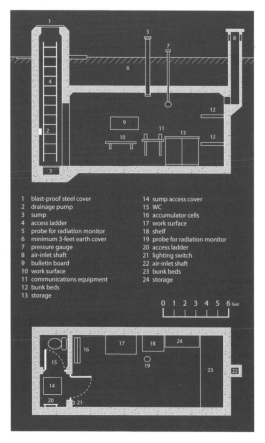

1 blast-proof steel cover
2 drainage pump
3 sump
4 access ladder
5 probe for radiation monitor
6 minimum 3-feet earth cover
7 pressure gauge
8 air-inlet shaft
9 bulletin board
10 work surface
11 communications equipment
12 bunk beds
13 storage
14 sump access cover
15 WC
16 accumulator cells
17 work surface
18 shelf
19 probe for radiation monitor
20 access ladder
21 lighting switch
22 air-inlet shaft
23 bunk beds
24 storage

0 1 2 3 4 5 6 feet

LEFT Plan and sectional views of a typical ROC monitoring post. *(Bill Padden)*

OPPOSITE TOP Typical 'Rotor' guardhouse. Some 350,000 tons of concrete, 20,000 tons of steel and thousands of miles of cabling for the telephone and telex connections were used to construct the network of 'Rotor' bunkers, radar installations, and command and control centres. *(Bill Padden)*

OPPOSITE BOTTOM Typical 'Rotor 3' operations room. Designed to detect aircraft as small as a jet fighter at a range of 200 miles (320km) and an altitude of 50,000ft (15,240km), 'Rotor 3' would have extended coverage across Northern Ireland, and the north and north-west of Scotland, but was never completed. *(Bill Padden)*

ABOVE Headquarters building for ROC number 15 group at Fiskerton, Lincolnshire. The building was commissioned in 1960 and closed in 1992. *(Nick Catford)*

RIGHT Headquarters building for ROC number 7 group at Bedford. Note the near identical construction to the Fiskerton building: both feature a semi-underground design. *(Historic England)*

'Rotor 2' saw the new 'Green Garlic' Type 80 radar system installed on 29 existing sites. And, although it was never fully completed, 'Rotor 3' would have extended coverage across Northern Ireland, and the north and north-west of Scotland, allowing even fighter aircraft to be detected at a range of 200 miles (320km) and an altitude of 50,000ft (15,240km). Additionally, 'Rotor 4' consisted of sector operational command (SOC) sites at Barnton Quarry, Bawburgh, Kelvedon Hatch and Shipton. Work on 'Rotor' ended in February 1956.

Advances in jamming techniques, and the emergence of other electronic countermeasures (ECM), suggested that new radar equipment would be necessary to continue to provide adequate early warning of attack. In February 1961, what had originally been described as 'Plan Ahead' was approved for deployment under the name 'Linesman'. The new system was to be integrated with civil air-traffic control, with elements of the latter designated 'Mediator'. The new, more-powerful Marconi Type 84

LEFT Guardhouse and entrance to the bunker at Kelvedon Hatch, Essex. Decommissioned in 1992, the bunker served initially as an air-defence station before being converted to a 'Rotor 4' site in 1953, and subsequently served as a Regional Seat of Government (RSG). The standard design of the guardhouse can also be seen at other, similar, sites. *(Nick Catford)*

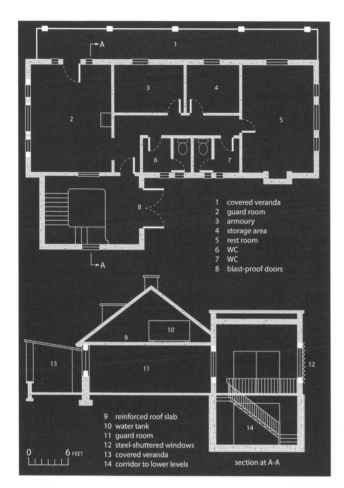

1 covered veranda
2 guard room
3 armoury
4 storage area
5 rest room
6 WC
7 WC
8 blast-proof doors

9 reinforced roof slab
10 water tank
11 guard room
12 steel-shuttered windows
13 covered veranda
14 corridor to lower levels

section at A-A

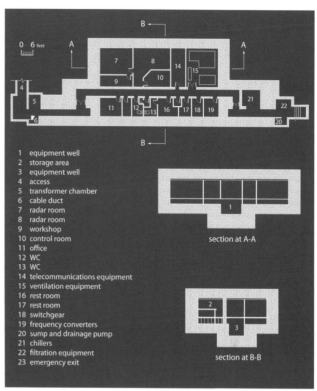

1 equipment well
2 storage area
3 equipment well
4 access
5 transformer chamber
6 cable duct
7 radar room
8 radar room
9 workshop
10 control room
11 office
12 WC
13 WC
14 telecommunications equipment
15 ventilation equipment
16 rest room
17 rest room
18 switchgear
19 frequency converters
20 sump and drainage pump
21 chillers
22 filtration equipment
23 emergency exit

section at A-A

section at B-B

ABOVE 'Rotor 1' consisted of 34 'Chain Home' stations, 8 early warning stations, 11 underground control interception stations and 14 semi-submerged above-ground interception stations. The drawing shows a typical 'Rotor 1' operations room. *(Bill Padden)*

BELOW 'Rotor 4' sector operational command (SOC) installation. 'Rotor 4' sites were at Barnton Quarry, Bawburgh, Kelvedon Hatch and Shipton. *(Bill Padden)*

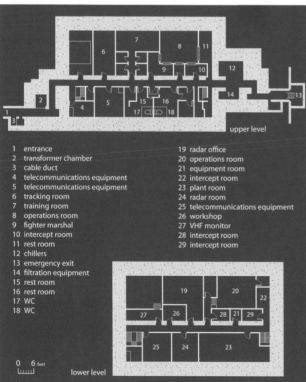

upper level

1 entrance
2 transformer chamber
3 cable duct
4 telecommunications equipment
5 telecommunications equipment
6 tracking room
7 training room
8 operations room
9 fighter marshal
10 intercept room
11 rest room
12 chillers
13 emergency exit
14 filtration equipment
15 rest room
16 rest room
17 WC
18 WC

19 radar office
20 operations room
21 equipment room
22 intercept room
23 plant room
24 radar room
25 telecommunications equipment
26 workshop
27 VHF monitor
28 intercept room
29 intercept room

lower level

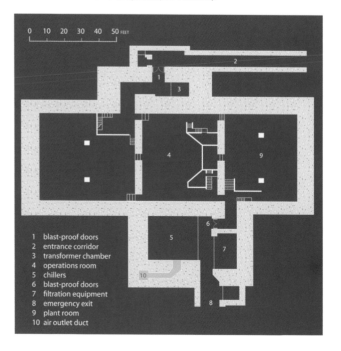

1 blast-proof doors
2 entrance corridor
3 transformer chamber
4 operations room
5 chillers
6 blast-proof doors
7 filtration equipment
8 emergency exit
9 plant room
10 air outlet duct

ABOVE Marconi 'Linesman' Type 84 radar array at RAF Neatishead, Norfolk. Replacing the earlier 'Rotor' system, 'Linesman' operated on a wavelength of 230mm using a 60ft (18.3m) wide antenna reflector. The transmitting equipment was contained in the building on which the aerial was mounted.
(Warehouse Collection)

radar equipment was installed at three sites, in Norfolk, Northumberland and North Yorkshire, and, unlike the earlier 'Rotor' system, 'Linesman' incorporated central control using a mainframe computer operating across a local area network.

By 1968, the further-improved AEI 'Blue Yeoman' Type 85 radar, designed to deter hostile jamming by rapidly changing

RIGHT Element of the war telephone system at RAF Neatishead; this is the equipment that would have been used to issue the 'four-minute warning'.
(Warehouse Collection)

frequencies, was installed at all three stations, complete with heavy-duty cooling equipment. 'Linesman' was finally declared fully operational in 1974, by which time it was considered to be vulnerable to Soviet stand-off missiles. By this time, NATO had moved away from the so-called 'tripwire' response, typified by 'Rotor' and 'Linesman', and was investigating a more flexible warning system incorporating both deterrent and defence components.

In 1971, a NATO report entitled 'A Revised Plan for the UKADGE', proposed centralising command at West Drayton and High Wycombe, with control and reporting centres at RAF Buchan (Scotland), Neatishead (Norfolk), Bishops Court (Northern Ireland) and Boulmer (Northumberland). At the same time, early warning radar and control systems were deployed in Shackleton aircraft based at Kinloss and Lossiemouth in Scotland to provide 'over-the-horizon' coverage. The ground sites were linked by a narrow-band digital ring main that allowed one station to provide backup should others suffer technical problems or be damaged by enemy action, while the UK Air Defence Ground Environment (UKADGE) system was fully integrated with the wider NATO Air Defence Ground Environment (NADGE) system.

By 1972, the NADGE system had evolved into the NATO Integrated Air Defense System

ABOVE Standard local early warning and control (SLEWC) consoles and tote board at RAF Neatishead. *(Nick Catford)*

RIGHT The Marconi S600 transportable long-range radar system was designed for early warning and surveillance, control of surface-to-air missiles, coast watching and military air-traffic control. The equipment could be air-lifted by helicopter, loaded into transport aircraft such as the C130 or towed by a Land Rover. *(Warehouse Collection)*

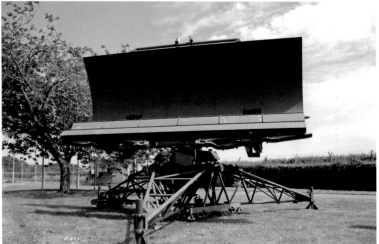

(NATINADS), consisting of 84 radar sites and associated control centres across Europe, including sites in Britain. This, in turn, became the airborne early warning/ground environment integration segment (AEGIS) in the early 1980s, assembling and interpreting data derived from both AWACS and NATINADS into visual displays.

RIGHT Staxton Wold was first used as a radar station in 1937, as part of the 'Chain Home' system, and is the oldest continuously serving radar station in the world. The station was one of those equipped with Type 84 radar, but, by 1996, this had been removed and replaced with Plessey Type 93 equipment removed from RAF Hopton. *(Nick Catford)*

'Pressing the nuclear button'

Whilst it is one thing developing an effective early warning system, it is quite another to react to the data received and to actually 'press the nuclear button'.

In the USA, the President has the final say over the deployment of nuclear weapons, with the launch codes of what is described as the Single Integrated Operational Plan on hand at all times. The President is always accompanied by a military aide who carries the so-called 'nuclear football', a name which dates back to Eisenhower's time, and an attack plan code-named Operation Dropkick. The 'football' is actually a small leather briefcase containing a book listing classified site locations, a description of procedures for the Emergency Alert System that allows the President to address the nation and a small plastic card on which are printed the authentication codes – described as the 'Gold Codes' – required to launch a strike. The launch codes, and the equipment used for decrypting them, are generated daily by the National Security Agency.

The orders to retaliate against any perceived Soviet threat would be issued through one of the USA's underground command, control and communications centres. Six of these facilities were constructed during the 1950s as part of a programme that also included a network of nuclear-bomb-proof bunkers to protect the major figures in the administration. The largest of these was the NORAD headquarters buried deep in the Cheyenne Mountain complex at Colorado Springs. From 1974, there was also an airborne command centre, designated 'Looking Glass', operating from a fleet of four modified Boeing 747 'Night Watch' airliners. A similar ground-based system is located at the National Airborne Operations Center at Offutt Air Force Base, Omaha, and there was an underground complex at Raven Rock Mountain in Pennsylvania, often described as the 'underground Pentagon'.

Unless co-ordination with the US Strategic Air Command is required, Britain's deterrent is under the control of the Prime Minister, through the Chief of the Defence Staff. By 1957, Britain had identified a list of 131 Soviet cities with a population exceeding 100,000, of which 98 had been selected as legitimate targets. Should the moment have arrived, the Prime Minister, or his designated survivor, would have issued the order, known as the 'letter of last resort', which, for much of the Cold War period, would have come from the underground bunker complex

CLEARANCE 10FT 5IN

at Corsham, Wiltshire, known as 'Burlington'. Should an attack have been deemed likely, a defined protocol allowed a civil servant to speak to the Prime Minister, whose responses would have been either: to retaliate, to not retaliate, for the commander to use his own judgement or to place himself under US or Australian command if possible.

By the end of the Cold War era, Britain had two control and reporting centres, one at Buchan, the other at Neatishead. These centres reported to the UK Combined Air Operations Centre at RAF High Wycombe where Strike Command headquarters was located until 2007. However, any orders to launch a 'Trident' strike from the British *Vanguard* submarine fleet would have been relayed to the operations room at the British military headquarters at Northwood, Hertfordshire, where the Chief of the Defence Staff would effectively have 'pressed the button'.

Exactly how the Soviet Union might have issued any orders to launch nuclear weapons remains unclear, but, since 1967, the Soviets are said to have developed an automatic 'trigger system' – often described as a 'Doomsday machine' – that would launch ballistic missiles if a nuclear strike were to be detected by seismic, light, radioactivity and overpressure sensors. Code-named 'Dead

ABOVE The bunker in which the NORAD headquarters is located is designed to withstand a 30-megaton nuclear blast within 1.2 miles (2km). Sets of 25-ton blast-resistant doors are used to protect the access tunnels. *(USAF)*

Hand', or 'Perimeter', this would allow the Soviets to maintain a retaliatory second-strike capability even if all of the High Command, and the Soviet underground command and control network deep under Moscow, had been incapacitated. Some small comfort can perhaps be gained from the fact that the system was only to have been made active during periods of heightened tension.

BELOW Photographed in May 1999, this is the vandalised remains of the guardhouse to the 'Rotor 1' station at Bempton, Yorkshire, which was commissioned in 1956. *(Nick Catford)*

Chapter Four

Air-launched nuclear weapons

━━━━(●)━━━━

Hiroshima and Nagasaki were attacked from the air using free-fall bombs, and for the next decade aircraft provided the only feasible means of delivery for strategic nuclear weapons. Both sides constructed long-range heavy bombers capable of delivering a nuclear payload across a distance, and maintained a fleet of such aircraft ready to fly at short notice.

'Someday, not too distant, there can come streaking out of somewhere – we won't be able to hear it, it will come so fast – some kind of gadget with an explosive so powerful that one projectile will be able to wipe out completely this city of Washington.'

General Hap Arnold, US Army, 1943

OPPOSITE Making its maiden flight in August 1952, the iconic Vulcan bomber provided the means of delivering Britain's nuclear deterrent from July 1956 to June 1969, when the role passed to the 'Polaris'-equipped submarines of the Royal Navy. *(Sergeant David S. Nolan; USAF)*

the long-range bomber, and, although the USA, Russia and China all continue to maintain a fleet of strategic bombers, the British V-Bombers had all been withdrawn from service by the mid-1980s, with the last remaining examples converted to air-to-air refuelling tankers.

The British V-Bombers

Development of Britain's V-Bomber fleet – the Vulcan, Valiant and Victor – started in January 1947, when the Air Ministry issued a specification for an advanced jet-powered, medium-range bomber that would be capable of carrying one 10,000lb (4,535kg) bomb to a target 1,720 miles (2,775km) distant. The specification stated that the aircraft must have a cruising speed of 575mph (925km/h), and be capable of flying at a ceiling of 50,000ft (15,200m).

Handley Page and Avro both responded with innovative designs. The Handley Page Victor featured crescent wings, whilst the Avro Vulcan used an even more advanced, visually striking, delta-wing arrangement with no tail-plane. Both companies received development contracts, the thinking being that if one of these advanced designs failed, the other would serve as useful insurance, and work on the two aircraft began at the end of 1947. A third, more conventional aircraft, the Vickers Valiant, was also commissioned in April 1948, following a less-demanding specification. Production of the three aircraft – collectively described as the V-Bomber force – started in the 1950s, with the intention of producing a fleet of 144 aircraft that could 'strike a worthwhile blow against our enemies', or, as the 1954 'Statement on Defence' put it, would be 'capable of using the atomic weapons to the fullest effect'.

By the middle of the next decade, Bomber Command had V-Bomber bases across the country, with the aircraft able to reach targets in the east of the Soviet Union, and in Warsaw Pact countries, in the shortest possible time. Valiants were stationed at RAF Marham, although they were soon withdrawn due to technical problems; there were nine Vulcan squadrons, at Cottesmore, Waddington and Scampton; and four Victor squadrons, at Honington, Wittering and Finningley, the latter a training unit. During the 1970s, there were

ABOVE Entering service with USAF Strategic Air Command in 1955, the Boeing B-52 Stratofortress is a long-range, subsonic, jet-powered strategic bomber constructed to carry nuclear weapons, and designed to provide a first strike or retaliation capability. *(US Department of Defense)*

All of Britain's independent nuclear weapons, including 'Blue Danube', 'Red Beard, 'Yellow Sun' and WE177, were free-fall bombs, designed to be dropped from the V-Bomber fleet. During periods of heightened tension, the USA kept squadrons of B-52 Stratofortress aircraft airborne around the clock, flying across the Atlantic to the coast of Europe and back, ready to retaliate against the Soviet Union.

Soviet bombers, including the Tupolev Tu-4 and the later Tu-16, described by NATO as 'Bull' and 'Badger', respectively, maintained the ability to strike against distant targets in Europe and the USA. The Chinese produced a licensed version of the Tu-16, known as the Xian H-6, equally capable of delivering nuclear weapons across thousands of miles. But, by the end of the 1950s, the development of more capable ICBMs had started to usurp the role of

BELOW Serving the Soviet Air Force between 1954 and 1993, the Tupolev Tu-16, code-named 'Badger' by NATO, was a twin-engined long-range strategic bomber designed to carry either free-fall bombs or air-launched nuclear or conventional cruise missiles. *(US Department of Defense)*

also Vulcan nuclear squadrons at RAF Akrotiri in Cyprus, although by this time responsibility for Britain's nuclear deterrent had theoretically passed to the Royal Navy.

For two decades, the RAF took its role as the defender of Britain extremely seriously, maintaining aircraft at a high state of readiness.

Vickers Valiant

Despite the fact that work on the Vickers Valiant B1 had started last, it was actually the first of the new strategic jet-powered bombers to take to the air, making its maiden flight on 18 May 1951. Designed for a crew of five, consisting of the pilot and co-pilot, air electronics officer (AEO), navigator radar officer and navigator plotter, the Valiant was capable of carrying 21,000lb (9,535kg) of conventional weapons, or a single 10,000lb (4,535kg) free-fall nuclear weapon such as 'Blue Danube' or 'Red Beard', or the American Mks 5, 7, 15, 28 and 43 nuclear bombs. Four Rolls-Royce Avon jet engines were buried in the wing root, and the Valiant was able to deliver its payload across 4,500 miles (7,245km) – more than enough to get to the heart of the Soviet Union and back from bases in Britain. Maximum speed was 567mph (913km/h), and the aircraft had an operating ceiling of 49,000ft (14,700m).

The Valiant entered service in 1955, with a total of 100 examples constructed. There were four sub-variants, including photo-reconnaissance aircraft, which entered service in 1955, and in-flight refuelling tankers, the first of these entering service a year later, in

1956; seven Valiants carried ECM equipment. In 1956, during Operation Buffalo, a Valiant dropped the first British nuclear weapon at the Maralinga site that formed part of the Woomera range in Australia. A year later, in 1957, during Operation Grapple, a Valiant tanker was adapted to drop 'Short Green Granite', Britain's first thermonuclear (hydrogen) bomb, at Malden Island and Christmas Island in the Central Pacific Ocean.

By 1960, it was not possible for aircraft to fly high enough to avoid interception and the RAF's strategy changed to low-level bombing. The Valiant proved unable to withstand the additional stresses imposed by low-level flying, and was withdrawn in 1965, when fatigue cracks were discovered in the main wing spar.

Avro Vulcan

Designed by Roy Chadwick and Stuart Davies, the prototype Avro 698, later to become the Vulcan, made its maiden flight on 30 August 1952. The first production example, the Vulcan B1, flew on 4 February 1955, and the type entered service in May 1956.

ABOVE The Vickers Valiant was the first V-Bomber to enter service with the RAF, but, like the Victor, it was withdrawn prematurely from its intended role when fatigue cracks started to appear in the main wing spar.
(Air Team Images)

LEFT WZ391 was one of 11 examples of the Valiant photo-reconnaissance aircraft, and served with 543 Squadron at RAF Gaydon. The aircraft was photographed at the Battle of Britain at Home Display at Edinburgh in 1958, two years after delivery.
(Air Team Images)

RIGHT The unmistakeable delta-wing shape of the Avro Vulcan, in this case a B2 variant, showing the low-level glossy Medium Sea Grey and Dark Green disruptive pattern camouflage that was adopted for the upper surfaces from the mid-1960s. *(Air Team Images)*

BELOW Finally retired at the end of the 2015 season, Vulcan XH558 was the last surviving airworthy example of this fine aircraft. It was also the last Vulcan to fly in military service and was one of six Vulcans converted to the aerial refuelling tanker role. *(Air Team Images)*

The prototype was powered by four Bristol Avon jet engines, but once production of the B1 variant started, these were changed to Bristol (later Rolls-Royce) Olympus engines, providing almost double the power. Late production variants had a maximum speed of 644mph (1,038km/h), a service ceiling of 55,000ft (16,775m) and a range of 2,607 miles (4,171km). The wing of the prototypes, and of the B1 variant, was a pure delta shape, but when the improved Vulcan B2 appeared in 1960, this had been changed to a compound design, often described as the 'kinked wing'. Operated by a crew of five, the Vulcan was a very capable aircraft, and it was said to be able to outmanoeuvre an F-15 fighter in a high-altitude mock dogfight.

Production of the Vulcan continued until 1965, with a total of 136 examples constructed, including two prototypes, at an average unit cost of £750,000 each, and the type formed the backbone of Britain's airborne nuclear deterrent for much of the Cold War, carrying 'Blue Danube', 'Violet Club' and 'Yellow Sun' Mk 1 or Mk 2 free-fall nuclear bombs. The Vulcan was also capable of carrying conventional weapons. There were 45 examples of the B1, 30 of

LEFT The Vulcan was capable of carrying 'Blue Danube', 'Green Grass', Mk 5, 'Red Beard', 'Violet Club', 'Yellow Sun' and WE177 nuclear weapons. The aircraft could also deploy the 'Blue Steel' stand-off missile following modifications to the bomb bay. *(US Department of Defense)*

which were subsequently converted to carry ECM equipment; these started to enter service in 1960. The remaining aircraft were of B2 configuration, 24 of which were subsequently converted to carry the 'Blue Steel' 1.1-megaton air-launched stand-off missile. The conversion entailed cutting away the bomb-bay doors, as well as various internal modifications, but these aircraft were withdrawn and converted back to B2 configuration in 1970 when the use of 'Blue Steel' was discontinued. Four B2 variants were converted for maritime radar reconnaissance in 1973, and, in 1982, six B2s were rebuilt as air-to-air refuelling tankers, with fuel tanks in the bomb bay.

Early production examples were finished in silver, but this was changed to an anti-flash white paint to help reflect the thermal radiation from a nuclear explosion. However, the possible effects of nuclear flash, of both light and heat, on the crew remained a very real issue. In a slightly surreal official film, the crew are shown wearing single eye-patches: if the initial brilliant flash of light produced by the nuclear detonation resulted in blindness of the exposed eye, whether permanent or temporary, the patch could be removed and the pilot could continue to fly the aircraft using the other eye. Anti-flash goggles were subsequently developed to provide better protection.

With the introduction of a low-level attack strategy in the mid-1960s, many aircraft were refinished with a glossy disruptive camouflage pattern on the upper surfaces, consisting of a sea-grey background with dark green stripes. The undersurfaces generally remained white,

although, in 1979, a number of aircraft were painted an all-over camouflage pattern.

The Vulcan was used operationally on just one occasion, during the Falklands War in 1982, and the last examples were withdrawn from service in 1984. One airworthy aircraft has survived – although it ceased flying at the end of 2015 due to the high cost of maintenance.

Handley Page Victor

Designed by Reginald Stafford, the Handley Page HP80 Victor was the third, and most advanced, of the V-Bombers, and is readily identified by its crescent wings, thick wing roots and distinctive air intakes. The prototype made its maiden flight on Christmas Eve 1952, and the first production example flew on 1 February 1956. The aircraft entered service at the end of 1957, and a total of 84 examples were constructed before the production line was

ABOVE 'Blue Steel' air-to-surface nuclear stand-off missile being offloaded from its AEC Mandator transporter vehicle on to a trailer that will allow it to be manoeuvred under an aircraft for loading. The missile required up to seven hours of launch preparation, with refuelling alone taking some 30 minutes, and it was said to be highly unreliable. *(IWM, RAF-T 4863)*

LEFT 'Blue Steel' missile being readied for loading under a Vulcan bomber; the size of the missile prevented it fitting inside the bomb bay and it was carried under the fuselage. Entering service in 1963, the missile carried a 'Red Snow' thermonuclear warhead with a yield of 1.1 megatons, and was finally retired in 1970. *(IWM, RAF-T 4855)*

ABOVE The Handley Page Victor was designed to carry 'Blue Danube' and 'Yellow Sun' weapons; like the Vulcan, it could also be converted to carry a single underslung 'Blue Steel' stand-off missile. *(Air Team Images)*

closed down in 1963. Like the Vulcan and the Valiant, the Victor was capable of carrying either a conventional payload, in this case in the form of thirty-five 1,000lb (450kg) bombs, or a single 'Blue Danube'. The bomb bay was sufficiently large to be able to carry four of the later 'Red Beard', 'Yellow Sun' Mk 1 or Mk 2 bombs.

In its early B1 form, the Victor was powered by four Armstrong-Siddeley Sapphire jet engines, but, by the time the improved B2 variant, with its extended wingspan, appeared in 1961, the engines were Rolls-Royce Conway units, with a Blackburn Artouste auxiliary engine in the right-hand wing root. Capable of operating at a ceiling of 56,000ft (17,080m), the B1 variant had a maximum speed of 626mph (300km/h), and a range of 6,000 miles (9,720km).

A total of 84 Victors were constructed, 50 of the original B1 configuration, with the remainder being the later B2. Numbers of

CENTRE Making its first flight in 1952, and entering service in 1958, the Victor was the last of the three V-Bombers. It was withdrawn from the nuclear role in 1968, when fatigue cracks were discovered in the wing structure, exacerbated by use of the aircraft as a low-level bomber. *(Air Team Images)*

LEFT A total of 84 Victors were constructed, 50 of which were of the original B1 variant, the remainder being the more powerful B2, which can be recognised by its larger air intakes. *(Air Team Images)*

and the casings were stored separately. For the fissile cores, 57 small brick and concrete kiosks were constructed, known as 'hutches' or 'igloos': 48 'Type A' hutches, each holding a single core, and nine 'Type B' hutches, each holding two cores. Combination locks were fitted to the 'hutches' to prevent unauthorised access, and each core was stored in a 2ft (610mm) deep, lidded stainless-steel vessel set into a borehole in the solid concrete floor. The maximum storage capacity was 64 cores, although it seems that this was never reached.

The casings, the high-explosive components and other non-nuclear items were kept in three larger brick-built buildings, protected by earth banking. Each of these buildings was provided with a 10-ton lifting gantry for handling the large and heavy 'Blue Danube' bombs – the casing was 24ft (7.32m) long and 60in (1,524mm) in diameter, and the complete weapon weighed 10,000lb (4,636kg). The facility also included maintenance and workshop areas, a fire station, guardroom and an administration block.

Although Barnham was some way from the V-Bomber airfields, the site supplied assembled weapons to RAF Cottesmore, Gaydon, Honington, Marham, Waddington, Wittering and Wyton. However, within less than a decade it had become obvious that nuclear-weapon storage facilities should be provided at the airfields themselves. The 'hutches' at Barnham were decommissioned in 1963, and the property was sold in 1966. Parts have been redeveloped, but some of the original buildings and kiosks remain, and the site has been scheduled as a monument by Historic England.

ABOVE LEFT Inside each hutch, the fissile core was stored in a stainless-steel vessel cast into the concrete floor slab. The building was protected by a combination lock, but the heavy counterbalanced lid to the storage vessel had nothing more than a simple cam lock. *(Warehouse Collection)*

ABOVE The 'Type B' hutches at Barnham, of which there were nine, included provision for storing two fissile cores. *(Warehouse Collection)*

Similar storage and maintenance facilities were also constructed at a former heavy bomber base at RAF Faldingworth, Lincolnshire, in 1957, to supply the northern V-Bomber bases at Coningsby, Finningley and Scampton.

BELOW RAF Barnham is now a small industrial estate, but the hutches and many of the other buildings, including the three earth-protected structures where the high-explosive components and other non-nuclear items were stored, still remain. *(Warehouse Collection)*

ABOVE By 1964, the standard British nuclear bomb was the WE177, for delivery by air as a bomb or as a helicopter-launched depth charge. Physically smaller than previous weapons, it was manufactured in three variants: WE177A, with a yield between 0.5 and 10 kilotons; the 450-kiloton WE177B; and the 200-kiloton WE177C. *(IWM, MUN 004664)*

The site started to be run down from 1968, and was deactivated by 1972; it is currently used as an industrial estate.

By 1964, the standard British nuclear bomb was the WE177. Physically smaller than previous weapons, WE177 was manufactured in three variants, and was stored, assembled and maintained on the V-Bomber bases in earth-covered concrete 'special weapons' stores on the airfields. Eventually, the bombs were kept in underground vaults inside the hardened shelters, thus reducing time spent on loading, and further shortening reaction time.

ABOVE Sectioned WE177A round at Boscombe Down Aviation Collection, near Salisbury. The weapon is 112in (2,845mm) long and weighs 600lb (272kg). A total of 107 examples of the 'A' variant were constructed. *(Brian Burnell)*

ABOVE Road trials of the WE177 using a purpose-designed four-wheeled trailer attached to a Series I Land Rover; 1965, Farnborough. *(RAF Museum, Crown Copyright)*

BELOW South bomb store at RAF Upper Heyford, one of a number of secure weapons' storage facilities on the site. From 1950, Upper Heyford was home to elements of the USAF Strategic Air Command intercontinental bombing force, consisting of B-36 and B-50 bombers. *(Historic England)*

BELOW HAS at RAF Honington, with ground equipment annexe. Built from reinforced materials with concrete panel doors, the 128ft (39m) long HAS was constructed to a standard NATO design, and was designed to protect aircraft on the ground from both conventional and nuclear attack. *(Historic England)*

US air-launched nuclear weapons

Since the original 'Little Boy' and 'Fat Man' weapons of 1945, the USA has developed more than 30 types of free-fall nuclear bomb, with yields ranging from a relatively modest 1 kiloton to a massive 25 megatons, designed to be delivered by long-range strategic bomber aircraft (see Table 7, below).

'Little Boy' and 'Fat Man' were both dropped from modified B-29 Superfortress aircraft, but the size and weight of the weapons made them difficult to deploy. By 1947, the B-29 had been superseded by the B-36 Peacemaker and then by the B-50, an intercontinental bomber that was purpose-designed to deliver nuclear weapons. The first jet-powered strategic bomber was the B-47 Stratojet, which appeared in 1950, but it is the turbojet-engined B-52 Stratofortress that is most closely associated with the air-dropped nuclear weapons of the Cold War. Introduced in 1954, the B-52 has already clocked up an incredible 60 years in service, with examples still flying to the present day

TABLE 7 US NUCLEAR FREE-FALL BOMBS IN SERVICE, 1945–83

Date in service	Name and/or designation*	Description and warhead	Yield
1945	Mk 1 'Little Boy'	Free-fall bomb; uranium fission warhead	15–16 kilotons
1945	Mk 3 'Fat Man' Model Y-1561	Free-fall bomb; plutonium fission warhead	21 kilotons
1949	Mk 4 'Fat Man'	Free-fall bomb; fission warhead	1–31 kilotons
1951	Mk 6	Free-fall bomb; fission warhead	8–160 kilotons
1951	Mk 8 'Elsie'	Free-fall earth-penetrating weapon; fission warhead	25–30 kilotons
1952	Mk 5	Free-fall bomb; fission warhead	6–120 kilotons
1952	Mk 7	Free-fall bomb; fission warhead	8–61 kilotons
1953	Mk 18 'Super Oralloy'	Free-fall bomb; fission warhead	500 kilotons
1954	Mk 12 'Brok'	Free-fall bomb; fission warhead	12–14 kilotons
1954	Mk 17, EC 17	Free-fall bomb; thermonuclear fusion enriched-lithium warhead	10–15 megatons
1954	Mk 24, EC 24	Free-fall bomb; thermonuclear fusion enriched-lithium warhead	10–15 megatons
1954	Mk 14, EC 14, TX 14	Free-fall bomb; thermonuclear fusion enriched-lithium warhead	5–7 megatons
1954	Mk 16, TX 16	Free-fall bomb; cryogenic thermonuclear fusion warhead	6–8 megatons
1955	Mk 15, TX 15	Free-fall bomb; thermonuclear fusion warhead, enriched-uranium casing	1.7–3.8 megatons
1955	Mk 21	Free-fall bomb; thermonuclear fusion warhead	4–4.5 megatons
1956	Mk 11	Free-fall earth-penetrating weapon; enriched-uranium fission warhead	25–30 kilotons
1956	Mk 36	Free-fall bomb; thermonuclear fusion warhead	6–19 megatons
1957	Mk 39	Free-fall bomb; thermonuclear fusion warhead	3–4 megatons
1958	Mk 105 'Hotpoint'	'Lay-down' parachute-suspended free-fall bomb; fission warhead	11 kilotons
1958	Mk 27	Free-fall bomb; thermonuclear fusion warhead	2 megatons
1958	Mk 28 series	Free-fall bomb; thermonuclear fusion warhead	0.07–1.45 megatons
1960	Mk 41, B41	Free-fall bomb; thermonuclear fusion warhead	25 megatons
1961	Mk 43, B43	'Lay-down' parachute-suspended free-fall bomb; thermonuclear fusion warhead	0.07–1 megaton
1962	Mk 53, B53	Free-fall bunker-buster bomb; thermonuclear fusion warhead	9 megatons
1963	Mk 57, B57	Free-fall lightweight bomb/depth bomb; fission warhead	5–20 kilotons
1968	B61	Free-fall or parachute-suspended multipurpose bomb; thermonuclear fusion warhead	0.3–340 kilotons
1983	B83	Free-fall multipurpose bomb; thermonuclear fusion warhead	1.2 megatons

* Other designs were developed and assigned sequence numbers but were not necessarily put into production.

TABLE 8 US AIR-LAUNCHED NUCLEAR WEAPON SYSTEMS IN SERVICE, 1957–90

Date in service	Name and designation	Warhead	Description	Range	Yield
Air-launched guided missiles					
1956	'BOAR'	W7	Air-to-surface rocket; fission warhead	7.5 miles (12km)	20 kilotons
1957	'Genie' (AIR-2)	W25	Air-launched missile; fission warhead	6 miles (10km)	1.5 kilotons
1957	'Rascal' (GAM-63)	W27	Air-to-surface ballistic missile; thermonuclear fusion warhead	100 miles (162km)	2 megatons
1959	'Bullpup' (AGM-12C)	W45	Air-to-ground missile; fission warhead	12 miles (20km)	1–15 kilotons
1961	'Falcon' (AIM-26A)	W54	Air-to-air guided missile; fission warhead	6 miles (10km)	0.25 kilotons
1962	'Skybolt' (GAM-87)	W59	Air-launched ballistic missile; thermonuclear fusion warhead	1,150 miles (1,850km)	1 megaton
1972	SRAM (AGM-69A)	W69	Air-to-surface short-range missile; fission or thermonuclear fusion warhead	35–100 miles (56–160km)	17–210 kilotons
Air-launched cruise missiles					
1960	'Hound Dog' (AGM-28)	W28	Air-to-air tactical cruise missile; thermonuclear fusion warhead	700 miles (1,134km)	0.5–4 megatons
1982	ALCM (AGM-86B)*	W80-1	Air-launched cruise missile; thermonuclear fusion warhead	1,500 miles (2,400km)	5–150 kilotons
1990	ACM (AGM-129A)	W80-1	Advanced air-launched cruise missile; thermonuclear fusion warhead	2,000 miles (3,250km)	5–150 kilotons

* AGM-86B cruise missiles remain in US service as of 2016.

BELOW The last flight of the USAF B-47 Stratojet bomber, which was retired in 1986. Introduced in 1950, the Stratojet was the world's first jet-powered strategic bomber, and acted as the first line of America's nuclear deterrent. Many were operated from forward bases in Britain and elsewhere. *(US Department of Defense)*

(2016), and is expected to remain in US service until 2045.

As the weapons became smaller, more aircraft, including many fighters, were also considered to be 'nuclear capable'. Later US

RIGHT Mk 28 thermonuclear bomb being unloaded from USAF Boeing B-52H Stratofortress aircraft during Exercise Global Shield 84. There were 20 versions of the Mk 28, with yields varying between 0.07 and 1.45 megatons. *(US Department of Defense)*

nuclear bombers include the B-58 Hustler, the A-5 Vigilante, the FB-111 Aardvark and the B-2A Spirit stealth bomber.

Air-launched guided missiles

The first air-to-surface nuclear missile deployed by the USA was the Bureau of Ordnance atomic rocket ('BOAR'), an unguided ballistic stand-off weapon. Developed for the US Navy, and entering service in 1956, the 30.5in (775mm) diameter 'BOAR' was armed with a 20-kiloton W7 warhead, and had a range of 7.5 miles (12.1km). From April 1959, it was superseded by 'Bullpup', and all examples had been withdrawn from service by 1963. 'Bullpup' was also a stand-off weapon, but had an extended range of 12 miles (20km), and was armed with a 1–15-kiloton W45 warhead, or 1,000lb of conventional explosive. The improved 'Bullpup A' was introduced in 1960, with a total of more than 22,000 examples constructed; this was superseded by 'Bullpup B', but both types had been withdrawn by 1976.

ABOVE 'Bullpup B' was a stand-off air-to-surface weapon, with a range of 12 miles (20km), armed with a 1- to 15-kiloton W45 warhead. *(USAF)*

LEFT Entering service in 1957, 'Rascal' was a strategic missile designed to give otherwise obsolete bombers a stand-off attack capability. With a range of around 100 miles (162km), the missile was armed with a 2-megaton W27 thermonuclear warhead. *(USAF)*

(160km). The missile entered service in 1957, with the last example withdrawn just two years later.

In the late 1950s, development work started on 'Skybolt', an air-launched ballistic missile capable of delivering a 1-megaton W59 warhead across a range of 1,150 miles (1,860km). The missile was not successful, and a series of failures during testing led to its cancellation in December 1962. This caused a political storm in Britain as all its other projects had been cancelled in favour of the purchase of 'Skybolt', which Britain had planned to deploy in the V-Bomber fleet. Work had already been done on a number of Vulcans to allow 'Skybolt' missiles to be carried outboard of the wing landing gear. Britain was eventually offered 'Polaris' in its place and the converted Vulcans were modified to accept US 'Shrike' air-to-surface missiles designed for use against radar and communications targets.

The short-range attack missile (SRAM) filled the gap left by the cancelled 'Skybolt' project, and provided the USAF with an air-to-surface nuclear missile armed with a W69 warhead that had a 17-kiloton yield in fission mode and 210 kilotons in fusion mode. SRAM was the smallest strategic nuclear weapon

ABOVE Inert SRAM being loaded to a USAF Rockwell B-1B heavy strategic bomber. *(US Department of Defense)*

Unlike 'BOAR', which had been developed for naval use, 'Rascal' was a strategic missile designed to give otherwise obsolete bombers a stand-off attack capability. Armed with a 2-megaton W27 thermonuclear warhead, 'Rascal' had a range of around 100 miles

BELOW B-52F long-range bomber taking off with its complement of two 'Hound Dog' cruise missiles mounted under the wings. 'Hound Dog' was introduced in 1959, and carried a W28 thermonuclear warhead with a variable 0.5- to 4-megaton yield. *(US Department of Defense)*

carried by US aircraft, and 20 missiles could be accommodated in a single B-52 along with four Mk 28 free-fall bombs with a variable 0.07 to 1.45-megaton yield. The operating range was 100 miles (160km) when fired at high altitude, and 35 miles (56km) at low altitude. Production began in 1971, with the first examples delivered in March the following year. SRAMs were withdrawn in June 1990.

Cruise missiles

Originally described as 'aerial torpedoes', cruise missiles are fitted with small wings and are designed to travel at a more or less constant velocity, either subsonic or supersonic. The missiles can be launched from air, land, surface ship or submarine, and are generally directed at distant tactical targets on land or at sea. Modern electronic guidance systems provide a high degree of accuracy.

'Hound Dog' was the first cruise weapon to be deployed by a USAF bomber, and was introduced into service in 1959, carrying a W28 thermonuclear warhead with a variable 0.5- to 4-megaton yield. Two 'Hound Dogs' could be carried underslung beneath a B-52, giving the aircraft the ability to attack two separate radar installations or surface-to-air missile sites, whilst remaining out of range. 'Hound Dog' continued in service for more than 15 years, with the last example removed from the front line in 1975; a number were retained in the USA's nuclear stockpile until 1978.

Development of the 'air-launched cruise missile' (ALCM) began in January 1968; it was originally intended as a decoy weapon that could confuse enemy radar into believing that it was 'seeing' a B-52 bomber. By 1973, the project had evolved into a nuclear-armed long-range cruise missile carrying a 200-kiloton W80-1 warhead. A single B-52 bomber was able to carry 20 ALCMs on wing pylons, as well as four Mk 28 bombs. Production began in January 1977, and, by 1980, the original ALCM had been superseded by a larger version with an extended range, although the number of missiles carried by the B-52 was reduced to ten.

The last production example was delivered in October 1986, and ALCM was eventually replaced by the 'advanced cruise missile', similarly armed with a W80-1 warhead with a variable yield of 5 to 150 kilotons, but providing greater range and a minimal radar signature. Deliveries began in June 1990, ending in August the following year.

BELOW The ALCM entered production in 1977. A single B-52 bomber could carry 20 ALCMs, each with a 200-kiloton W80-1 warhead, as well as four Mk 28 nuclear bombs. *(US Department of Defense)*

> 'To make our contribution to the deterrent we must ourselves possess the most up-to-date nuclear weapons, and the means of delivering them.'
>
> **Winston Churchill, speech in the House of Commons, 1 March 1955**

Chapter Five

Land-based nuclear weapons

'Little Boy' and 'Fat Man' were complex, physically large and relatively heavy weapons, and there was no alternative but to deliver them by air using specially modified aircraft. The size of the weapons meant that it would not have been possible for more than one to be carried, even if more had been available at the time, and land-based delivery across even a short distance was not feasible. Immediately after the end of the Second World War, the USA started to research the miniaturisation and standardisation of nuclear warheads, in order both to simplify their deployment and to allow the use of alternative delivery methods.

OPPOSITE Introduced into service in Europe in 1954, the truck-mounted 'Honest John' was the US Army's first nuclear-capable surface-to-surface missile. Examples served with the Royal Artillery between 1959 and 1976. *(Warehouse Collection)*

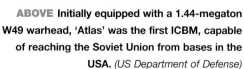

ABOVE Initially equipped with a 1.44-megaton W49 warhead, 'Atlas' was the first ICBM, capable of reaching the Soviet Union from bases in the USA. *(US Department of Defense)*

ABOVE RIGHT Typical Soviet ballistic missile – the OTR-22 (designated SS-12 by NATO), a short-range rocket with a yield of 500 kilotons, designed to be launched from its MAZ-543P TEL vehicle; May 1968. *(Warehouse Collection)*

RIGHT Introduced in 1988, towards the end of the Cold War, the Soviet 'Topol' RT2-PM (SS-25) ICBM carries a single 800-kiloton warhead. The TEL vehicle is the MAZ-7917. *(One Half 3544)*

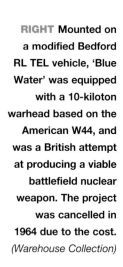

RIGHT Mounted on a modified Bedford RL TEL vehicle, 'Blue Water' was equipped with a 10-kiloton warhead based on the American W44, and was a British attempt at producing a viable battlefield nuclear weapon. The project was cancelled in 1964 due to the cost. *(Warehouse Collection)*

By the early 1950s, the USA had developed tactical warheads that could be incorporated in artillery shells and rockets; medium-range missiles soon followed and, by the beginning of the 1960s, the first ground-launched ICBMs started to appear in service in the form of the 'Atlas' rocket. Large numbers of different delivery vehicles capable of surface-launching megaton nuclear warheads against both civilian and military targets have subsequently been developed.

Britain, on the other hand, despite having successfully developed independent nuclear warheads and a fleet of bombers capable of visiting apocalypse on the Soviet Union, has been unable to bring any home-grown ground-launched nuclear delivery systems into service, either for the tactical or strategic role. 'Blue Streak', for example, was a medium-range ballistic nuclear missile on which work was started in the mid-1950s, but which was terminated before reaching production as being too expensive. Similarly, 'Blue Water', a surface-to-surface battlefield nuclear missile – that was also intended for use in the, similarly abandoned, TSR2 strike aircraft – was cancelled in April 1962, before being put into production. From the mid-1950s, the British Army deployed US-designed 'Honest John' missiles, followed by 'Corporal' and 'Lance', all of them armed with US-controlled nuclear warheads. Britain had also planned to use 'Skybolt' before the Americans cancelled it

in favour of the submarine-launched 'Polaris' and the subsequent 'Trident'.

US nuclear artillery

Nuclear artillery allowed the destructive power and deterrent effect of nuclear weapons to be exploited on the battlefield. The development of the first such weapon – dubbed 'Atomic Annie' – started in 1949, with the first test carried out in May 1953 at the Nevada Test Site. Officially designated M65, 'Atomic Annie' was a 280mm rifled cannon capable of delivering a 15-kiloton W9 nuclear projectile across a range of 20 miles (32km); the cannon

LEFT 'Blue Streak' was an attempt at building a British medium-range ballistic nuclear missile, but the project was cancelled in 1960 as being too expensive. The rocket component was subsequently used as the first stage of the Europa space carrier vehicle, and is seen here on the launch pad at Woomera in 1964. *(RAF Museum, Crown Copyright)*

LEFT 'Atomic Annie' was a 280mm artillery piece capable of firing a 15-kiloton W9 nuclear projectile across a range of 20 miles (32km). The size of the weapon was such that it required a pair of specially designed Kenworth tractors to move it from one location to another. *(Warehouse Collection)*

The USA unilaterally withdrew its nuclear artillery shells from service in 1991, and these weapons have generally been superseded by mobile tactical ballistic missiles.

The smallest tactical nuclear weapon developed by the USA was the M28/M29 recoilless spigot gun designed for use against tanks and ground forces. Nicknamed 'Davy Crockett' or 'the atomic rifle', the gun was designed to fire an M388 projectile carrying a W54-2 nuclear warhead, with a yield between 0.01 and 0.02 kilotons. Production began in 1956, with 2,100 examples constructed; the device remained in service until 1968.

Nuclear demolition munitions

Atomic demolition munitions (ADM) were 'dirty' nuclear weapons developed by the US Army in the first two decades of the Cold War. Designed for use in Europe in the event of Soviet invasion, ADMs would have been deployed by retreating units to destroy roads and bridges, and to contaminate key communication routes, preventing their use by the invading army – a technique known as 'area denial'. The smallest of the demolition munitions, the special atomic demolition munition (SADM), employing the 1-kiloton version of the W54 warhead, could just about be carried in a backpack, whilst the largest was armed with a 20-kiloton W7 or W31 warhead. The last weapons of this type were the W45-equipped medium atomic demolition munition (MADM) of 1965, which remained in service or storage until about 1987, and the W54-equipped SADM, which had been dismantled by 1992.

ABOVE Work on 'Atomic Annie' started in 1949, with the first test firing in 1953. Although a total of 20 cannon were produced, and the equipment was deployed to Europe and Korea, the weapon was withdrawn in 1963. *(Warehouse Collection)*

was 84ft (25m) in length, and required a pair of specially designed tractors to move it from one location to another. A total of 20 cannon were produced and were deployed to Europe and Korea, but the system was withdrawn in 1963. Nuclear shells were also produced for the M110 and M115 howitzers, using the lower-yield W33 and W79 warheads, and for the 155mm M114 and M198 howitzers, in this case deploying the W48 warhead. The nuclear-capable M110 howitzer was also deployed by Heavy Regiments of the Royal Artillery in Germany.

US tactical nuclear weapons

As would have been the case with atomic artillery, the use of tactical nuclear missiles would, initially, seem to be self-defeating since the resulting radiation would render areas of the battlefield hazardous for both sides. Nevertheless, in September 1947, the US Navy Board of Ordnance started the development of what eventually became 'Lacrosse', a truck-launched tactical missile designed to supplement conventional field artillery, and capable of carrying either a nuclear or a conventional warhead. The

BELOW Developed in the late 1950s for use against Soviet personnel and against armoured vehicles, the M28/M29 recoilless rifle, code-named 'Davy Crockett', was the smallest nuclear weapon deployed by the US Army, with a warhead of just 0.01–0.02 kilotons. *(US Department of Defense)*

RIGHT In September 1947, the US Navy Board of Ordnance started the development of what eventually became 'Lacrosse', a truck-launched tactical missile capable of carrying either a nuclear or a conventional warhead. Entering service in 1959, the nuclear-equipped 'Lacrosse' carried a 10-kiloton warhead. *(US Department of Defense)*

CENTRE Truck-mounted 'Honest John' missile elevated to the firing position. With a range of 15 miles, 'Honest John' carried a 20-kiloton W7 warhead, or the later 30-kiloton W31. It was also capable of delivering a conventional payload. *(Warehouse Collection)*

range was just 12 miles (20km), and the weapon was guided by a forward observation post mounted on a Jeep. Testing began in 1954, but the difficulties encountered meant that the first missile did not enter service until July 1959. In its nuclear-equipped form, 'Lacrosse' carried a 10-kiloton W40 boosted-fission warhead. Almost 1,200 examples were constructed, but all had been withdrawn by 1964.

The problems with the 'Lacrosse' project meant that the first US-designed surface-to-surface missile to enter service that was actually capable of carrying a nuclear payload was 'Honest John'. Properly designated 'artillery rocket XM31' and later simply 'M31', 'Honest John' was a fin-stabilised unguided device similar to the German V2 of the Second World War. It was able to deliver either a 20-kiloton W7 warhead, or the later 30-kiloton W31; non-nuclear payloads included 1,500lb (682kg) of conventional explosive, or the M190 chemical cluster warhead carrying M134 or M139 sarin bomblets. The range was just 15 miles (25km), and the missile was designed to be launched from a truck-mounted ramp. The first example was tested during late June 1951, with production of some 7,000 missiles starting in 1952. 'Honest John' battalions were deployed in Europe in early 1954, and the missile served with 15 nations, including Britain, Belgium, France and West Germany, with the nuclear warheads under what was described as 'two-key' control, meaning that a US authentication officer was always in attendance before launch. The last examples were withdrawn in 1985.

LEFT Without the missile in place, the 'Honest John' TEL launcher vehicle, designated M289 or M386 (the latter with a shorter launch ramp), was air-portable in the USAF Douglas C-124 Globemaster transport aircraft. *(US Army)*

ABOVE 'Honest John' was effectively made obsolete by the introduction of 'Corporal', a tactical guided missile capable of carrying either a 20-kiloton W7 warhead or 1,500lb of conventional explosive across 87 miles (140km). The photograph shows a development version of the weapon, together with the smaller 'Private' experimental rocket that was used to help develop the concept of fin-stabilisation. *(NASA/JPL-Caltech)*

BELOW 'Corporal' missile on its distinctive transporter-erector (TE) vehicle; once the missile was readied for launch, the vehicle was withdrawn. The Royal Artillery deployed two 'Corporal' regiments in West Germany from the mid- to late 1950s. *(Warehouse Collection)*

'Honest John' remained in service for a total of 30 years, despite the fact that, in 1954, it was effectively rendered obsolete by the development of the 'Corporal' short-range tactical missile. Designed by a partnership of the Firestone Tire and Rubber Company, Gilfillan Brothers, the Douglas Aircraft Company and the Jet Propulsion Laboratory at Caltech, 'Corporal' was capable of carrying either a 20-kiloton W7 nuclear-fission tactical warhead or 1,500lb of conventional explosive across a range of 87 miles (140km). The use of a ground-based guidance system made it the first example of an American guided weapon, although 'Corporal 2' was introduced in 1956 in an attempt to solve problems with the guidance system. The weapon remained in service until 1963, with some 1,100 examples constructed. A number were supplied to Britain from 1956 and were deployed by Guided Weapons Regiments of the Royal Artillery, again with the nuclear warheads under 'two-key' control.

A lightweight version of 'Honest John' was tested in 1956, under the designation 'Little John' and armed with a 10-kiloton W45 warhead. It was the smallest nuclear-capable rocket deployed by the US Army, and two 'Little John' rockets could be carried in a standard 6 x 6 truck. The weapon was designed to be launched from a special trailer, and the complete rocket and trailer assembly could be moved to the launch site by Jeep. Few were constructed, however, and the weapon was withdrawn in August 1969.

Designed to supersede 'Corporal', 'Sergeant' was a short-range, surface-to-surface solid-fuel tactical ballistic missile with an inertia guidance system. The designated warhead was the 200-kiloton W52, developed especially for this application, and the range was between 25 and 85 miles (40–135km). 'Sergeant' entered production in 1962, and was deployed overseas by the following year, but, by 1972, it had been replaced by 'Lance', a tactical ballistic missile able to deliver either a 100-kiloton W70 nuclear warhead, or a conventional high-explosive payload. Between 1981 and 1992, the 1-kiloton W70-3 enhanced-radiation warhead was also used, being particularly effective against armoured vehicles. 'Lance' was the last battlefield nuclear weapon deployed by the US

RIGHT Test firing of the 'Sergeant' short-range, surface-to-surface tactical ballistic missile at White Sands in 1961. Carrying a 200-kiloton W52 warhead, 'Sergeant' was designed to supersede 'Corporal', and had a range of 25 to 85 miles (40–135km). *(US Department of Defense)*

Army, and was also deployed by 50th Missile Regiment, Royal Artillery.

Deployment of the surface-to-air 'Nike Hercules' began in 1958, to provide a medium- and high-altitude long-range air-defence weapon for NATO and US forces. Based on the world's first anti-aircraft missile system, 'Nike', which dated from 1953, the two-stage 'Nike Hercules' was intended to deliver a 20-kiloton W31 nuclear warhead, although early examples were equipped with a W7 warhead. Nuclear-

BELOW By 1972, 'Sergeant' had been replaced by the 100-kiloton 'Lance' missile, seen here being readied for test firing. 'Lance' was also deployed by 50th Missile Regiment, Royal Artillery. *(US Department of Defense)*

BELOW RIGHT Mounted on the M752 self-propelled mobile launch vehicle, 'Lance' was the last battlefield nuclear weapon deployed by the US Army. *(IWM, CT-001210)*

ABOVE Introduced into service in 1952, 'Matador' carried a 40–50 kiloton W45 nuclear warhead and was equipped with a radar-directed radio guidance system. It was the first cruise missile to be deployed by the USAF, with 1,200 examples constructed. *(US Department of Defense)*

BELOW Derived from the earlier 'Nike' anti-aircraft missile, 'Nike-Hercules' was a medium- and high-altitude long-range air-defence weapon carrying a 20-kiloton W31 nuclear warhead; early examples were equipped with a W7 warhead. *(US Department of Defense)*

armed 'Nike Hercules' missiles were deployed in the USA, as well as with the Greek, Italian, South Korean and Turkish Armies, under 'two-key' control; the missile was also deployed by Belgian, Dutch and US forces in West Germany. 'Nike Hercules' had been completely withdrawn by 1988.

Cruise missiles

Although more generally deployed from aircraft and shipping, ground-launched cruise missiles (GLCM) have been in the US nuclear arsenal since the introduction of the Martin MGM-1 'Matador' in 1952. Carrying a 40–50 kiloton W45 nuclear warhead, 'Matador' was similar to the German V1 flying bomb of the Second World War, but was equipped with a radar-directed radio guidance system that allowed course corrections to be made during flight. A total of 1,200 examples were built, the last leaving service in 1962.

Making its first appearance in service in the 1970s, the McDonnell Douglas BGM-109 'Tomahawk' was a ground-launched, all-weather medium- to long-range, low-altitude land-attack cruise missile capable of deploying both conventional and nuclear warheads. The guidance system, used in conjunction with either 'inertial and terrain contour matching' radar guidance and optical 'digital scene matching area correlation' data, or with GPS satellite navigation and on-board programming, allowed extremely accurate targeting, and its relatively small size made radar detection difficult. The BGM-109A variant, development of which started in 1980, carried a W80 thermonuclear warhead with a yield variable between 5 and 150 kilotons, whilst the BGM-109G 'Gryphon' variant used a W84 warhead, with a yield between 0.2 and 150 kilotons.

In the 1980s, RAF Molesworth and Greenham Common were selected as the British bases for 160 'Gryphon' cruise missiles,

LEFT Ground-launched 'Tomahawk' cruise missiles were introduced in the 1970s, with a guidance system that allowed precise targeting of individual targets with minimal collateral damage, even through heavily defended airspace. *(Raytheon)*

RIGHT BGM-109G 'Gryphon' cruise missile equipped with a W84 warhead, with a yield between 0.2 and 150 kilotons. Four missiles are carried in launch tubes mounted on a semi-trailer that provides a TEL facility. *(Technical Sergeant Rob Marshall; US Department of Defense)*

leading to nearly a decade of civilian protest. These, and other ground-launched nuclear-armed cruise missiles, were withdrawn from service in 1991 to comply with the Intermediate-Range Nuclear Forces Treaty, but a quantity of W84 warheads remain in storage.

US strategic nuclear weapons

High-yield strategic nuclear weapons are designed to be used against military targets such as command centres, factories, missile launch sites, and communications and early warning facilities, as well as against towns and cities. Early weapons of this type were deployed from aircraft, but, by the mid-1950s, the use of medium-, and eventually long-range, ballistic missiles had started to become the norm, the first of these in the form of 'Snark', a long-range cruise missile with a yield of 4 megatons.

In 1958, the 'Jupiter' medium-range missile was introduced, capable of delivering a 1.44-megaton W49 warhead across a distance of 1,500 miles (2,400km). Some 200 'Jupiter' missiles were constructed, and around a quarter

BELOW Test firing of a 'Gryphon' cruise missile. The missiles were deployed to six locations across Europe, including RAF Molesworth and RAF Greenham Common, where they attracted considerable protest. *(US Department of Defense)*

LEFT Test launch of the 'Snark', a long-range cruise missile with a yield of 4 megatons. The weapon entered service in 1957. *(US Department of Defense)*

ABOVE Rocket engine for the 'Jupiter' medium-range ballistic missile; developing a thrust of around 150,000lbf (667kN) for around three minutes, the Rocketdyne S-3D motor allowed 'Jupiter' to deliver its 1.44-megaton W49 warhead across a distance of 1,500 miles (2,400km). *(Rocketdyne)*

miles (14,500km); the W49 was eventually superseded by the 3.75-megatons W38.

Development of the 'Thor' intermediate-range ballistic missile (IRBM) had started in 1956/57 in response to fears that the Soviet Union was gaining the upper hand in the arms race; with a range of 1,750 miles (2,820km), 'Thor' was more than capable of delivering the 1.44-megaton W49 warhead to the Soviet capital from bases in Britain. By 1958, under the code name Project Emily, 'Thor' had become part of an Anglo-American agreement that placed the missiles with RAF Bomber Command at four converted wartime airfields, each with four satellite stations and a deployment of 15 missiles; the first site, at RAF Feltwell in Norfolk, became operational in August 1958. During the Cuban Missile Crisis, 59 of these weapons, at RAF bases at Bardney, Caistor, Coleby Grange, Folkingham, Hemswell and Ludford Magna, were brought to operational readiness, edging the world very close to nuclear war. The sites remained active until September 1963, when the missiles were decommissioned and returned to the USA.

As a possible backup in the event of the 'Atlas' project being delayed, the two-stage 'Titan 1', an early variant of the rocket used during the 'Gemini' space programme, was

of this number were deployed to bases in Italy and Turkey, but all 'Jupiter' missiles had been withdrawn by 1963, as part of a *quid pro quo* agreement with the Soviet Union regarding missiles in Cuba. From 1959, the same W49 warhead was initially fitted to the intercontinental 'Atlas', with the range now extended to 9,000

RIGHT During the late 1950s, the USA was concerned that the Soviet Union was 'winning' the arms race. The response was 'Thor', an intermediate-range ballistic missile with a range of 1,750 miles (2,820km), which could deliver its 1.44-megaton W49 warhead to the Soviet capital from bases in Britain. *(USAF)*

FAR RIGHT During the Cuban Missile Crisis, in October 1962, 59 'Thor' missiles were prepared for launch at their bases at RAF Bardney, Caistor, Coleby Grange, Folkingham, Hemswell and Ludford Magna. *(USAF)*

ABOVE 'Titan 2' photographed in its underground silo with the covers open ready for launch. *(US Department of Defense)*

RIGHT 'Titan 2' was an ICBM designed to carry a 9-megaton W53 warhead. The photograph was taken during a test launch at Vandenberg Air Force Base. *(USAF)*

pressed into service between early 1962 and mid-1965, deploying the familiar W38 or W49 warhead. The improved 'Titan 2' was a silo-based ICBM designed to carry a 9-megaton W53 warhead, and there were also plans to arm 'Titan 2' with a massive 35-megaton warhead, which would have been amongst the most powerful weapons deployed by the USA. All 350 'Atlas' missiles had been withdrawn by 1965.

'Atlas', 'Titan' and 'Thor' were eventually all replaced by the silo-based 'Minuteman': a three-stage liquid-fuelled rocket with a range of more than 8,000 miles (13,000km), initially designed to deliver a 1.2-megaton W56 warhead or a 1-megaton W59. Development of 'Minuteman' started in the late 1950s, with the first examples entering service in 1962, and the increased range meant that it was no longer necessary for American ballistic missiles to be based in Britain. By 1965, 'Minuteman 2' had been introduced, with a 1.2-megaton W56 warhead. The current 'Minuteman 3' entered service in 1970/71, carrying a W62 172-kiloton warhead, or up to three 300-kiloton W87 MIRV (multiple independently targetable re-entry vehicle)

warheads. 'Minuteman 3' was the first ballistic missile to use MIRV warheads, in which each warhead is able to seek a separate target after separation from the parent vehicle, resulting in a greater destructive effect for a given total yield, and reducing the effect of anti-ballistic missile measures. Thousands of missiles had been produced before production ended in December 1978, and at the time of writing (2016) 'Minuteman' is the only ICBM in the US nuclear arsenal, with some 450 examples in service.

'Minuteman 3' was to have been superseded by the MIRV-equipped 'Peacekeeper', designed to deliver ten W87-equipped re-entry vehicles, each with a yield of 300 kilotons. Some 50 missiles were deployed from 1986, but it was agreed that they would be retired in 2005 as part of the bilateral US–Russian Strategic Arms Reduction Treaty known as START II. The Treaty was never ratified, but all 'Peacekeeper' missiles had been decommissioned by September 2005, and,

TABLE 9
US NUCLEAR ARTILLERY AND DEMOLITION MUNITIONS IN SERVICE, 1953–65

Date in service	Name and designation	Warhead	Description	Range (where appropriate)	Yield
Nuclear artillery					
1953	–	W9, W19	280mm artillery shell for M65 'Atomic Annie' artillery; fission warhead	20 miles (30km)	15 kilotons
1957	XM422	W33	203mm artillery shell for M110 and M115 howitzer; fission warhead	8.75 miles (14km)	1–2 kilotons
1958	'Davy Crockett' M28, M29	W54	Nuclear shells for 120mm/155mm recoilless artillery; fission warhead	1.25–2.5 miles (2–4km)	0.01–0.02 kilotons
1963	M-454 AFAP	W48	155mm artillery shell for M114 or M198 howitzer; fission warhead	8.75 miles (14km)	1–2 kilotons
1981	M753	W79-0, W79-1	203mm artillery shell for M115 howitzer; fission warhead	18 miles (30km)	0.1–1.1, 0.8 kilotons
Nuclear demolition munitions					
1954	ADM	W7	Atomic demolition munition; fission warhead	–	20 kilotons
1957	ADM T4	W9 modified	Atomic demolition munition; fission warhead	–	15 kilotons
1958	ADM Mk 31	W31	Atomic demolition munition; fission warhead	–	20 kilotons
1960	SADM	W54	Special atomic demolition device; fission warhead	–	0.01–1 kiloton
1961	TADM 'Sewer Pipe' (XM113)	W30	Tactical atomic demolition munition; fission warhead	–	0.3–0.5 kilotons
1964	SADM Mk 54	W54	Special atomic demolition munition; fission warhead	–	0.01–1 kiloton
1965	MADM	W45	Medium atomic demolition munition; fission warhead	–	1–15 kilotons

TABLE 10
US GROUND-LAUNCHED NUCLEAR WEAPON SYSTEMS IN SERVICE, 1953–86

Date in service	Name and designation	Warhead	Description	Range	Yield
Tactical weapons					
1953	'Honest John' (MGR-1)	W7, W31	Surface-to-surface ballistic missile; fission or boosted-fission warhead	5–30 miles (8–48km)	2–30 kilotons
1955	'Corporal' (MGM-5)	W7	Surface-to-surface ballistic missile; fission warhead	87 miles (140km)	20 kilotons
1958	'Davy Crockett' M28, M29	W54	Recoilless artillery with nuclear shells; fission warhead	1.25–2.5 miles (2–4km)	0.01–0.02 kilotons
1958	'Nike Hercules' (MIM-14)	W7, W31	Surface-to-air ballistic missile; fission or boosted-fission warhead	90 miles (140km)	2–28 kilotons
1958	'Redstone' (PGM-11)	W39	Field artillery ballistic missile; thermonuclear fusion warhead	57 miles (92km)	3.5 megatons
1959	'Bomarc' (CIM-10)	W40	Surface-to-air guided missile; boosted-fission warhead	248 miles (400km)	7–10 kilotons

Date in service	Name and designation	Warhead	Description	Range	Yield
Tactical weapons (continued)					
1959	'Lacrosse' (MGM-18)	W40	Surface-to-surface ballistic missile; boosted-fission warhead	12 miles (20km)	10 kilotons
1960	'Pershing 1', 1A (MGM-31A)	W50	Field artillery ballistic missile; thermonuclear fusion warhead	460 miles (745km)	400 kilotons
1961	'Little John' (MGR-3)	W45	Surface-to-surface ballistic missile; fission warhead	12 miles (19km)	1–10 kilotons
1962	'Sergeant' (MGM-29A)	W52	Surface-to-surface ballistic missile; thermonuclear fusion warhead	85 miles (139km)	200 kilotons
1962	'Terrier' (RIM-2D)	W45	Surface-to-air ballistic missile; fission warhead	20 miles (32km)	1 kiloton
1970	'Sprint'	W66	Anti-ballistic missile; enhanced-radiation thermonuclear fusion warhead	25 miles (40km)	20 kilotons
1973	'Lance' (MGM-52)	W70, W70-3	Surface-to-surface ballistic missile; enhanced-radiation thermonuclear fusion warhead	45–75 miles (73–120km)	1–100 kilotons
1975	'Spartan' (LIM-49A)	W71	Anti-ballistic missile; thermonuclear fusion warhead	460 miles (740km)	5 megatons
1983	'Pershing 2' (MGM-31)	W85	Field artillery ballistic missile; thermonuclear fusion warhead	1,100 miles (1,800km)	5–80 kilotons
Cruise missiles					
1954	'Matador' (MGM-1)	W5	Surface-to-surface cruise missile; fission warhead	700 miles (1,135km)	40–50 kilotons
1957	'Snark' (SM-62)	W39	Surface-to-surface cruise missile; thermonuclear fusion warhead	6,300 miles (10,200km)	4 megatons
1959	'Mace' (MGM-13, CGM-13)	W28	Surface-to-surface cruise missile; thermonuclear fusion warhead	1,400 miles (2,270km)	2 megatons
1975	'Tomahawk' (BGM-109)	W80, W84	Surface-launched cruise missile; thermonuclear fusion warhead	1,725 miles (2,775km)	0.2–150 kilotons
1983	'Gryphon' (BGM-109G)	W84	Surface-launched cruise missile; thermonuclear fusion warhead	1,500 miles (2,430km)	0.2–150 kilotons
Strategic weapons					
1958	'Jupiter' (PGM-19)	W49	Surface-to-surface medium-range missile; thermonuclear fusion warhead	1,500 miles (2,400km)	1.44 megatons
1959	'Atlas' (SM-65)	W38, W49	Surface-to-surface ICBM; thermonuclear fusion warhead	9,000 miles (14,500km)	3.75, 1.44 megatons
1959	'Thor' Mk 7 (PGM-17)	W49	Surface-to-surface intermediate-range missile; thermonuclear fusion warhead	1,750 miles (2,820km)	1.44 megatons
1959	'Titan 1' (HGM-25A, SM-68)	W38, W49	Surface-to-surface ICBM; thermonuclear fusion warhead	6,300 miles (10,200km)	3.75, 1.44 megatons
1962	'Minuteman 1' (LGM-30)	W56, W59	Surface-to-surface ICBM; thermonuclear fusion warhead	8,000 miles (13,000km)	1.2, 1 megatons
1963	'Titan 2' (LGM-25C)	W53	Surface-to-surface ICBM; thermonuclear fusion warhead	9,325 miles (15,000km)	9 megatons
1965	'Minuteman 2' (LGM-30F)	W56	Surface-to-surface ICBM; thermonuclear fusion warhead	8,000 miles (13,000km)	1.2 megatons
1970	'Minuteman 3' (LGM-30G)	W62, 3 × W78*	Surface-to-surface ICBM; thermonuclear fusion warhead	8,000 miles (13,000km)	172, 3 × 340 kilotons
1986	'Peacekeeper' (LGM-118A)	12 × W87	Surface-to-surface ICBM; thermonuclear fusion warhead	8,700 miles (14,000km)	12 × 300–475 kilotons

* From 2007, 'Minuteman 3' missiles were retro-fitted with single 475-kiloton W87 warheads from obsolete 'Peacekeeper' missiles.

RIGHT Entering service in 1962, 'Minuteman' replaced 'Atlas', 'Titan' and 'Thor', and, with a range of more than 8,000 miles (13,000km), it was no longer necessary for American missiles to be based in Britain. Early examples were armed with either a 1.2-megaton W56 warhead, or a 1-megaton W59. *(US Department of Defense)*

BELOW It was originally planned that 'Minuteman' would be superseded by 'Peacekeeper', armed with up to ten re-entry vehicles, each carrying a 300-kiloton W87 warhead, as seen here, or a 475-kiloton W87-1/W88 warhead. *(US Department of Defense)*

BELOW RIGHT Test launch of 'Peacekeeper' ICBM. Around 50 missiles were deployed from 1986, but all had been decommissioned by September 2005 under the START II Strategic Arms Reduction Treaty. *(US Department of Defense)*

speaking at a final decommissioning ceremony, Dr Ronald M. Sega, Under-Secretary of the Air Force, credited 'Peacekeeper' with helping to end the Cold War. A number of W87 warheads taken from decommissioned 'Peacekeeper' missiles have been retro-fitted to 'Minuteman 3'.

Missile launch silos

Early missiles were stored in hangars or underground chambers and were prepared for launch using hydraulic lifts or ramps. The underground launch silo, which provides concealment as well as secure storage and launch facilities, offers a better solution, and the first example was designed in Britain in the 1950s for the 'Blue Streak' project. Constructed from 5ft thick (1.5m) steel-encased reinforced concrete, with a massive rail-mounted concrete lid, the silo was designed to withstand a 1-megaton blast, and to protect against electro-magnetic pulse during launch. The missile was stored upright in a U-shaped chamber that allowed the rapid exit of exhaust gas during the launch phase, and the silo also included fuel storage tanks at the base, together with six storeys of crew accommodation, control rooms, workshops and so on. A 1:60-scale model was constructed, as well as a 1:6-scale mock-up, but, of the 60 silos that were planned, work started on just one, at RAF Duxford, and this did not get beyond the making of trial boreholes before the project was abandoned.

RIGHT Typical 'Thor' missile site, one of 20 operated by the RAF from 1959, each with three missiles. The missiles were stored horizontally on TE trailers, under cover of a retractable shelter. Before the weapon could be fired, the shelter had to be retracted and the missile raised to an upright position; the entire launch sequence took about 15 minutes. *(Warehouse Collection)*

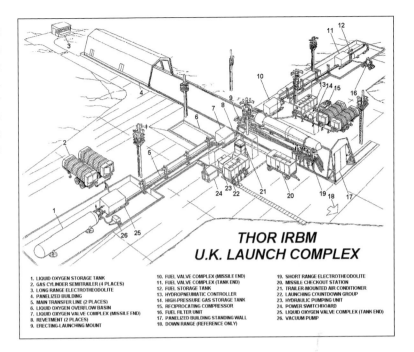

**THOR IRBM
U.K. LAUNCH COMPLEX**

1. LIQUID OXYGEN STORAGE TANK
2. GAS CYLINDER SEMITRAILER (4 PLACES)
3. LONG RANGE ELECTROTHEODOLITE
4. PANELIZED BUILDING
5. MAIN TRANSFER LINE (2 PLACES)
6. LIQUID OXYGEN OVERFLOW BASIN
7. LIQUID OXYGEN VALVE COMPLEX (MISSILE END)
8. REVETMENT (2 PLACES)
9. ERECTING-LAUNCHING MOUNT
10. FUEL VALVE COMPLEX (MISSILE END)
11. FUEL VALVE COMPLEX (TANK END)
12. FUEL STORAGE TANK
13. HYDROPNEUMATIC CONTROLLER
14. HIGH-PRESSURE GAS STORAGE TANK
15. RECIPROCATING COMPRESSOR
16. FUEL FILTER UNIT
17. PANELIZED BUILDING STANDING WALL
18. DOWN RANGE (REFERENCE ONLY)
19. SHORT RANGE ELECTROTHEODOLITE
20. MISSILE CHECKOUT STATION
21. TRAILER-MOUNTED AIR CONDITIONER
22. LAUNCHING COUNTDOWN GROUP
23. HYDRAULIC PUMPING UNIT
24. POWER SWITCHBOARD
25. LIQUID OXYGEN VALVE COMPLEX (TANK END)
26. VACUUM PUMP

In the USA, underground storage silos had been used since the introduction of 'Atlas' and 'Titan 1', but the missiles were stored horizontally, needing to be raised to a vertical position for launch. From about 1963, with the introduction of 'Titan 2', the rapid-launch underground silo was developed, allowing the missile to be fuelled, armed and launched from below ground. The silos were sited away from centres of population in Arizona, Colorado, Montana, Nebraska, North Dakota, South Dakota and Wyoming.

As of 2016, 'Minuteman 3' remains the USA's only silo-based missile system – housed in the same, now-ageing, 50-year-old silos that were constructed for 'Titan 2'.

LEFT Maintenance work being conducted on a 'Minuteman 2' in its underground launch silo. *(US Department of Defense)*

BELOW Diagram of a typical 'Titan' missile silo with the sliding cover open. Image taken from display board at the Titan Missile Museum, Tucson. *(Warehouse Collection)*

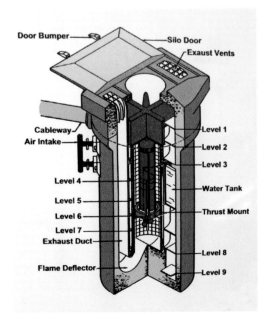

Door Bumper
Silo Door
Exaust Vents
Cableway
Air Intake
Level 1
Level 2
Level 3
Level 4
Water Tank
Level 5
Level 6
Thrust Mount
Level 7
Exhaust Duct
Level 8
Flame Deflector
Level 9

BELOW The 'Peacekeeper' missile was encased in a canister in the silo to protect it against damage. During launch, the missile was ejected by pressurised gas, with ignition occurring at a height of about 50ft (16m). *(US Department of Defense)*

Chapter Six

Naval nuclear weapons

Ship-launched nuclear weapons, including undersea missiles, depth charges, nuclear torpedoes and naval artillery, have been part of the standard nuclear arsenal of both sides since the mid-1950s. The British MoD, for example, has stated that it was 'routine practice for Royal Navy vessels to carry nuclear weapons during the 1980s'. Naval nuclear weapons came to the fore with the development of SLBM in the 1960s. Constantly on the move, the nuclear submarine is eminently 'survivable' as a launch pad, and is virtually immune from attack, making most other types of nuclear weapon obsolete.

OPPOSITE *Vanguard*-class submarine, HMS *Vigilant*, photographed at the Clyde Naval Base. Each of Britain's 'Trident'-equipped submarines is capable of carrying up to 16 missiles, with up to 12 nuclear warheads per missile; in 2010, the figure was reduced to 8 operational missiles and a maximum of 40 warheads. *(Ministry of Defence)*

'One has to look out for engineers
– they begin with sewing machines
and end up with the atomic bomb.'

French novelist, Marcel Pagnol

LEFT Early 'Polaris A1' on the launch pad. Although the first examples were test launched from Cape Canaveral, 'Polaris' was designed to be submarine-launched, with the A1 and A2 variants carrying a 600-kiloton W47 thermonuclear warhead across a 1,200-mile (1,900km) range. *(US Department of Defense)*

Early SLBMs had a relatively short range, necessitating operation from either the North Sea or the Mediterranean in order to reach the Soviet Union, but by the time the multiple-warhead 'Polaris A3' appeared in 1964, the type had evolved into a formidable weapon, capable of delivering its three 200-kiloton warheads across more than 2,800 miles (4,500km). 'Polaris', particularly in its improved 'A3TK' form, and later 'Trident', have provided Britain's major, and eventually only, nuclear deterrent.

Submarine-launched missiles

In 1960, the first example of 'Polaris', a two-stage solid-fuel submarine-launched rocket, described as a 'second-strike' weapon, was launched from Cape Canaveral, Florida, with the type entering service in 1961. The improved 'Polaris A2' offered a small increase in range, but by the time 'Polaris A3' appeared in 1964 the original 1,380-mile (2,235km) range had been more than doubled. 'Polaris A3' carried three 200-kiloton W58 thermonuclear warheads, but the examples that were supplied to Britain in 1962 ('Polaris A3T' and 'Polaris A3TK') were equipped with a British-designed fission-fusion-fission development of the W59 warhead known as ET317.

Most examples of 'Polaris' had been withdrawn from service by 1980, with the last 'Polaris A3' patrol taking place the following year. It was planned that 'Polaris' would be superseded by 'Poseidon', the first SLBM to be equipped with MIRV. Initial 'Poseidon' tests were conducted in August 1968, and the missile entered US service in 1971.

LEFT 'Polaris' warhead on display at the RAF Cold War Museum, Cosford. *(Warehouse Collection)*

RIGHT Royal Navy 'Polaris' at Cape Canaveral, **1988.** *(US Department of Defense)*

Subsequent quality-control and reliability problems, coupled with the failure of the missile to achieve its planned 4,000-mile (6,500km) range were never properly solved and the decision was taken to develop a new extended-range missile, using elements of 'Poseidon'. This eventually became 'Trident'.

Meanwhile, towards the end of the 1960s, the British government had initiated a project designed to improve 'Polaris' and to extend its life. Using the code name 'Super Antelope', and later 'Chevaline', the AWRE developed a modified 'Polaris' that also released dummy warheads, known as 'penetration aids', ensuring that sufficient of the multiple warheads from all of the missiles launched at one time would penetrate the enemy's anti-ballistic missile defence. Unfortunately, these improvements were at the expense of range, meaning that British SSBN (ship, submersible, ballistic, nuclear) submarines would be forced to operate closer to the Soviet Union, making them more vulnerable to countermeasures. However, the project was officially adopted by the government in 1974 and 100 warheads were produced, but, within five years, cost overruns had reached £1 billion. The improved 'Polaris A3TK' entered service in 1982 equipped with the redesigned multiple warheads, but two years earlier the decision had already been taken to eventually abandon 'Chevaline', replacing it with the American 'Trident' system.

Work on the development of 'Trident', a submarine-launched three-stage ballistic missile with a range in excess of 7,000 miles (11,340km), had started in 1971, initially described as the 'undersea long-range missile

RIGHT **'Trident 2' missile launched from a submerged Royal Navy submarine. 'Trident 2' was originally designed to deliver fourteen 100-kiloton W76, or 475-kiloton W88, warheads, but the number of warheads was restricted to eight under the START I Treaty of 1994.** *(US Department of Defense)*

Unarmed 'Trident 2' D-5 test launched from the USS *Nevada*.
(Seaman Benjamin Crossley; US Navy)

system', or 'extended range Poseidon'. The missile was designed to carry up to fourteen 100-kiloton W76, MIRV warheads, allowing US submarines to attack targets anywhere in the world. The system started to enter service in the USA in 1979, with the redesigned 'Trident 2' appearing in 1990. 'Trident 2' was similarly capable of delivering fourteen 100-kiloton W76 or 475-kiloton W88 warheads, but the number of warheads was restricted to eight under the conditions of the START I Treaty, which came into effect in 1994. Some US 'Trident 2' missiles were retro-fitted with W87 single warheads taken from obsolete 'Peacekeepers'.

In 1980, the British government announced that the Royal Navy would also adopt 'Trident', armed with warheads based on the W76 but produced at AWE. A total of 58 'Trident 2' missiles were leased to Britain, with the first submarine patrols taking place in 1994. Since 1998, 'Trident' has been the sole British nuclear weapon system, although the question of its eventual replacement in 2028 remains a topic of much discussion. Britain currently has the smallest nuclear arsenal of any of the five nations recognised as nuclear weapons states under the Nuclear Non-Proliferation Treaty, with just 58 missiles drawn from a pool owned by the USA, and is the only one of these states to rely on a single weapons system, described by the MoD as 'the minimum effective nuclear deterrent'.

Cruise missiles

The US Navy has deployed both 'Regulus' and 'Tomahawk' cruise missiles, launched from surface ships and submarines, with both capable of carrying either a conventional or nuclear warhead. 'Regulus' was the first US missile to be carried on a submarine, but, unfortunately, required the submarine to surface in order to effect a launch.

'Regulus' was in service between 1955 and 1964, and was armed with either a W5 or W27 warhead, the latter offering a maximum yield of 2 megatons. An improved 'Regulus 2' project was cancelled in 1958 in favour of 'Polaris'. 'Tomahawk' started to enter service in 1983, with nuclear variants carrying either the W80 or W84 warhead, each with a maximum yield of 150 kilotons. In 1995, a total of 65 'Tomahawk'

LEFT The replacement of the British 'Trident' programme continues to cause much controversy, although, in fact, it is the 'Trident'-equipped submarines that are being considered for replacement rather than the missiles themselves. (Campaign for Nuclear Disarmament)

ABOVE 'Tomahawk' cruise missile being launched from the submarine USS *Florida* in January 2003. 'Tomahawk' started to enter service in 1983. (US Navy)

LEFT Nuclear-equipped variants of the 'Tomahawk' cruise missile carry either the W80 or W84 warhead, each with a maximum yield of 150 kilotons. (US Department of Defense)

TABLE 11
US SHIP- OR SUBMARINE-LAUNCHED NUCLEAR MISSILES IN SERVICE, 1953–91

Date in service	Name and designation	Warhead	Description	Range	Yield
Submarine-launched guided missiles					
1960	'Polaris A1' (UGM-27)	W47	Submarine-launched ballistic missile; thermonuclear fusion warhead	1,200 miles (1,900km)	600 kilotons
1961	'Polaris A2' (UGM-27)	W47	Submarine-launched ballistic missile; thermonuclear fusion warhead	1,800 miles (2,800km)	600 kilotons
1964	'Polaris A3' (UGM-27)	3 × W58	Submarine-launched ballistic missile; thermonuclear fusion warhead	2,800 miles (4,600km)	3 × 200 kilotons
1967	'Polaris A3T'*	3 × ET317	Submarine-launched ballistic missile; thermonuclear fusion warhead	2,800 miles (4,600km)	3 × 200 kilotons
1971	'Poseidon' (UGM-73)	10 × W68	Submarine-launched ballistic missile; thermonuclear fusion warhead	2,800 miles (4,600km)	10 × 40 kilotons
1982	'Polaris A3TK'**	2 × ET317	Submarine-launched ballistic missile; thermonuclear fusion warhead	2,800 miles (4,600km)	2 × 225 kilotons
1979	'Trident 1' C4 (UGM-96A)	14 or 8 × W76	Submarine-launched ballistic missile; thermonuclear fusion warhead	4,600 miles (7,400km)	14 or 8 × 100 kilotons
1990	'Trident 2' D5 (UGM-133)***	14 or 8 × W88, W76	Submarine-launched ballistic missile; thermonuclear fusion warhead	4,800 miles (7,840km)	14 or 8 × 100, 475 kilotons
Ship- or submarine-launched cruise missiles					
1955	'Regulus 1' (SSM-N8)	W5, W27	Ship- or submarine-launched cruise missile; fission warhead	500 miles (810km)	40 kilotons, 2 megatons
1975	'Tomahawk' (BGM-109A)	W80, W84	Ship-launched surface-to-surface cruise missile; thermonuclear fusion warhead	1,725 miles (2,775km)	5–150 kilotons
Miscellaneous naval nuclear weapons					
1955	'Katie' Mk 23	W19, W23	16in naval shell for *Iowa*-class battleships; fission warhead	23 miles (35km)	15–20 kilotons
1955	'Betty' Mk 90	W7	Anti-submarine nuclear depth bomb; fission warhead	–	32 kilotons
1956	B57	W57	Anti-submarine nuclear depth bomb; fission warhead	–	5–20 kilotons
1958	B28	W28	Anti-submarine nuclear depth bomb; thermonuclear fusion warhead	–	0.07–1.45 megatons
1958	'Lulu' Mk 101	W34	Anti-submarine nuclear depth bomb; fission warhead	–	10 kilotons
1960	'Talos' (RIM-8D)	W30	Ship-launched surface-to-air or surface-to-surface missile; fission warhead	70 miles (112km)	5 kilotons
1961	ASROC (RUR-5A)	W44	Ship-launched anti-submarine stand-off missile; boosted-fission warhead	12 miles (19km)	10 kilotons
1963	ASTOR Mk 45	W34	Anti-submarine torpedo; fission warhead	10 miles (16km)	10 kilotons
1965	SUBROC (UUM-44A)	W55	Underwater-to-underwater missile; thermonuclear fusion warhead	25–35 miles (40–56km)	1.5 kilotons

* 'Polaris A3T' missiles in Royal Navy service are armed with a British-produced fission-fusion-fission warhead based on the American W59.

** Updated version of Royal Navy 'Polaris'.

*** 'Trident 2' missiles in Royal Navy service are armed with a British-produced warhead with a selective yield of 0.3, 5–10 or 100 kilotons, based on the American W76.

cruise missiles were supplied to the Royal Navy, although not equipped with nuclear warheads. Withdrawal of nuclear 'Tomahawks' started in the early 1990s, with the process completed by 2013.

Nuclear anti-submarine weapons

Nuclear depth bombs (NDB) are lightweight aerial weapons designed to explode underwater, destroying surface shipping and submarines by a powerful hydraulic shock. Most have a variable yield to allow their use at differing depths, or in positions close to land, and such weapons have been used by the Royal Navy, the US Navy and the Soviet Union. US-built devices include 'Betty', a 32-kiloton weapon equipped with the W7 warhead; 'Lulu', with a 10-kiloton W34 warhead; the B28 and B57 depth bombs, equipped with W28 and W57 variable-yield warheads, respectively; ASROC, with a W44 10-kiloton warhead; the ASTOR Mk 45 torpedo, using a 10-kiloton W34 warhead; and the stand-off SUBROC, a submarine-launched anti-submarine missile with a W55 warhead giving a yield of 1.5 kilotons. Of these, 'Lulu', as well as the B28 and B57 depth bombs, have been deployed by the Royal Navy and by NATO (see Table 11, page 108).

From about 1962 until 1972, the Royal Navy deployed a maximum of 35 'Red Beard' warheads as nuclear depth charges, eventually replacing them with WE177A warheads, delivered by Wasp, Lynx or Wessex helicopters, or dropped from Nimrod maritime patrol aircraft. The WE177 warhead was also fitted to the Australian-designed 'Ikara' ship-launched anti-submarine missile in Royal Navy service, in place of the conventional warhead, although there is some doubt as to whether or not any nuclear-armed 'Ikara' missiles were actually built.

During the 1982 battle to liberate the Falklands Islands it was reported that seven ships involved in the campaign, including HMS *Sheffield* and HMS *Coventry*, both of which were sunk as a result of enemy action, carried nuclear depth charges with WE177A warheads. The *Guardian* newspaper disclosed that two of the ships, HMS *Hermes*, the Royal Navy flagship during the campaign, and the

aircraft carrier HMS *Invincible*, carried 75% of the Navy's entire stockpile of nuclear depth charges. Despite refusing to comment on these reports for two decades, in 2003 the MoD finally admitted that British ships did possess nuclear weapons in the South Atlantic, but would not confirm which vessels were involved. In a statement, the MoD claimed that it was 'routine practice' for British naval ships to carry nuclear weapons during the 1980s, and that there was never any intention to use the weapons, which 'were already on board unnamed ships in the taskforce when it sailed'. Following the sinking of *Sheffield* and *Coventry*, the weapons were apparently returned to Britain 'in the ships with the best-protected magazines'.

If true, this put Britain in violation of the Tlatelolco Treaty of 1968 (Treaty for the Prohibition of Nuclear Weapons in Latin America and the Caribbean), which declared that all of South America should remain free of nuclear weapons, specifically banning 'the testing, use, manufacture, production or acquisition by any means whatsoever of any nuclear weapons', as well as prohibiting 'the receipt, storage, installation,

ABOVE B28 depth bomb training rounds; the weapon normally carries a variable-yield W28 warhead. *(US Department of Defense)*

BELOW In service with the Royal Navy, the Australian-designed 'Ikara' ship-launched anti-submarine missile (depth bomb) was modified to accept a WE177 nuclear warhead. *(IWM, MUN-085887A)*

ABOVE HMS *Repulse* was the first of four *Resolution*-class nuclear-capable submarines supplied to the Royal Navy from 1986. Each submarine was capable of carrying up to 16 'Polaris A3', and later 'Polaris A3TK', missiles, arranged in two rows of eight. *(Ministry of Defence)*

deployment and any form of possession of any nuclear weapons'. Protocol 1 of the Treaty binds overseas countries with territories in the region – including Britain, the USA, France and the Netherlands – to the terms of the Treaty.

All nuclear anti-submarine weapons were supposedly withdrawn from service by the five primary nuclear nations – the USA, Britain, France, the Soviet Union (Russia) and China – around 1990.

Resolution-class submarines

By the early 1960s it was clear that the British V-Bombers, armed with free-fall bombs and short-range stand-off missiles, were vulnerable to Soviet anti-aircraft activity and were

no longer able to provide an adequate deterrent. In May 1968, responsibility for providing Britain's nuclear deterrent passed from RAF Bomber Command to the ballistic missile submarines of the Royal Navy Submarine Service, with Britain's first ballistic missile submarine being the nuclear-powered *Resolution* class.

Based on the *Valiant*-class fleet submarine, the hull of the *Resolution* fleet was extended to 425ft (130m) to accommodate the missile compartment, with each submarine capable of carrying up to 16 'Polaris A3' missiles arranged in two rows of eight. It was originally planned that there would be five submarines (HMS *Resolution*, *Repulse*, *Renown*, *Revenge* and *Ramilles*), but, in the end, only four were actually constructed, with *Ramilles* cancelled in 1965 by a Labour government suddenly keen on saving taxpayers' money; nevertheless, the four ships together still cost more than £156 million.

The *Resolution*-class submarines were assigned to NATO, and operated out of a base at Faslane on the west coast of Scotland, with the vessels able to remain at sea undetected for months at a time. The first operational patrol took place on 15 June 1968, and during their near-30 years' service at least one *Resolution*-class submarine was always on patrol in what is still described as Operation Relentless, a 'continuous at-sea deterrence' programme. During the 1980s, all four *Resolution* submarines were converted to accept the 'Polaris A3TK' missile, carrying the British-manufactured 'Chevaline' MIRV warhead. *Resolution*-class submarines remained in service beyond the end of the Cold War, finally being replaced by the 'Trident'-equipped *Vanguard* class between 1994 and 1996. As the new submarines entered service, the old *Resolution*-class vessels were laid up at Rosyth Naval Dockyard prior to being cut up for scrap.

Britain's nuclear deterrent force currently (2016) consists of four *Vanguard*-class submarines, each originally capable of carrying up to 16 'Trident 2' D-5 ballistic missiles with up to 12 nuclear warheads per missile. This figure was reduced

LEFT HMS *Repulse* photographed in the Firth of Clyde in 1979, with the US Navy deep-sea rescue vehicle DSRV *Avalon*. *(US Department of Defense)*

LEFT From 1994, the older *Resolution*-class submarines were superseded by four new vessels described as the *Vanguard* class. Seen here in 1996, HMS *Vigilant* makes its way up the Clyde, with a complement of up to 16 'Trident 2' D-5 ballistic missiles, each carrying up to 12 nuclear warheads. *(Michael Storey; Ministry of Defence)*

to 8 operational missiles and a maximum of 40 warheads following decisions made in the 2010 'Strategic Defence and Security Review'.

Clyde Naval Base

Situated just 25 miles (40km) from Glasgow, on the eastern shore of Gareloch and north of the Firth of Clyde, Her Majesty's Naval Base (HMNB), Clyde, commonly referred to within the service as Faslane, is home to the Royal Navy's *Vanguard*-class nuclear-armed submarines. The location was selected for its easy access to the North Atlantic, and because it was close to the US Navy's SSBN base at Holy Loch, which operated until 1992.

Faslane was constructed as a naval base during the Second World War, when it was described as HMS *Neptune*, and the site became a shipbreaking yard after the war. In 1968, it was expanded to accommodate the 'Polaris'-equipped *Resolution*-class submarines, and, in the late 1980s, the north area of the site was enclosed by a high fence, with three jetties and a large ship-lift constructed for the new *Vanguard*-class submarines. The ship-lift can raise the 14,515-ton submerged weight of a *Vanguard* submarine in operational condition completely out of the water. Alongside the missile storage and maintenance facilities, there is a treatment plant for the disposal of nuclear waste from submarine reactors. Faslane has attracted considerable protest from those opposed to nuclear weapons, and has come in for genuine criticism for its safety record, with some 316 'nuclear safety events' reported over a five-year period. During

2013–14, there were six accidents on the site involving nuclear weapons.

The nearby Royal Naval Armaments Depot (RNAD) at Coulport is responsible for processing and maintaining the 'Trident' missiles and warheads. Although the missiles are generally returned to the USA for servicing, the warheads must be transported by heavily guarded road convoys to the AWE at Aldermaston. Coulport also includes facilities that enable missiles to be loaded into or removed from the submarines, as well as underground storage facilities for the missiles themselves. In addition to the facilities at Faslane and Coulport, *Vanguard*-class submarines are also repaired, refuelled and refitted at HMNB Devonport, near Plymouth, and, in 2002, a new refitting dock was constructed to support the work.

LEFT Photographed from the air, Her Majesty's Naval Base (HMNB), Clyde, is the current home of the Royal Navy's nuclear-capable *Vanguard*-class submarines, offering easy access to the North Atlantic and the US Navy's former SSBN base at Holy Loch. *(US Department of Defense)*

'Gentlemen, you can't fight in here! This is the war room.'

Peter Sellers speaking as President Merkin Muffley in _Dr Strangelove: or How I Learned to Stop Worrying and Love the Bomb_, 1964

Chapter Seven

Emergency government facilities

The British government was unable to provide fallout shelters for the population, but when it came to protecting the Establishment it was a different story. From the mid-1950s onwards, expensive concrete bunkers were constructed across the country providing sanctuary from which the Establishment believed it could conduct the war and subsequently direct survivors in rebuilding the nation. There were war headquarters, regional seats of government (RSG), command and communications bunkers, radar installations, county council shelters, local authority shelters, and hardened facilities for water board, electricity and telephone personnel.

OPPOSITE Located at the former RAF North Weald, the emergency centre for Epping Forest District Council remained in service until the mid-1990s, and was ultimately demolished in 2007. *(Nick Catford)*

The government couldn't dig deep enough, or pour the concrete thick enough, to ensure its own safety should the unthinkable have happened, and many of these subterranean facilities still remain, albeit now abandoned and neglected.

In the USA, some attempts were made to try to protect the civilian population should the worst occur, but, otherwise, it was the same story, with massive underground facilities excavated deep inside mountains for the military and the machinery of state. For example, an underground military centre and nuclear shelter was excavated 2,000ft (650m) inside Cheyenne Mountain, Colorado. Administration facilities were provided at a series of three-storey buildings deep inside Mount Weather, Virginia, to provide an alternate seat of civil government during a nuclear war. And, for the members of the House of Representatives and the Senate, a huge underground bunker was constructed beneath the Greenbrier Hotel at White Sulphur Springs, West Virginia, between 1959 and 1962, sufficient to house 1,600 personnel. The facility remained secret until 1992.

Central government facilities

In times of crisis or heightened tension, the business of central government in Britain would have been moved from Whitehall and Westminster Palace to the emergency government war headquarters (EGWHQ) at Corsham, Wiltshire. The 1962 'Cabinet Office War Book' describes how one of the code words that would have indicated to the Prime Minister that the moment had arrived to evacuate the government from London before a nuclear attack was, apparently, 'orangeade'.

At Corsham, buried deep beneath a series of disused Bath stone quarries, in part of a former wartime aircraft factory and ammunition store, an underground administrative complex had been constructed with around a million square feet (90,000m²) of office space. Initially described somewhat prosaically as 'Site 3', but later to be known as 'Burlington', work had started in 1940 to provide what was intended as a safe location in which to relocate between 4,000 and 7,500 central government personnel, including the Prime Minister, the Cabinet and key civil defence staff in the event of nuclear war. Interestingly, the fate of the royal family seems to remain undocumented.

The bunker was equipped with offices, storerooms, communications facilities, living and sleeping accommodation, kitchens, canteens, a TV studio and medical facilities. Sufficient fuel was available to allow the generators to run for three months, allowing personnel to be supported for a prolonged period, safe from whatever horrors were taking place above ground.

Although the site was far from complete, by 1960 there were facilities for around 1,500 staff. A year later, 'Site 3' became officially known as 'Burlington', and, by 1962, it is said that the complex was virtually finished, with only the telecommunications system still to be completed. By this time, the emphasis had changed, and 'Burlington' had been downgraded to house core government functions, as well as being the headquarters for the War Cabinet and the Chiefs of Staff. By the middle of the decade, 'Burlington' had become 'Turnstile', with all pretence at having a civil defence function abandoned. Some of the EGWHQ facilities were subsequently overhauled as part of the expansion of the UK Warning and Monitoring Organisations, and a section of the bunker was converted into a nuclear reporting cell. The facilities were upgraded between 1979 and 1982 in order to allow the bunker to operate as a 'command nucleus'

BELOW The so-called 'Main Road' in the government's 'Burlington' central war headquarters at Spring Quarry, Corsham. Construction work at this former underground aircraft factory started in November 1940.
(Nick Catford)

RIGHT **Area 12 kitchen at 'Burlington'. By 1960 the site included facilities for around 1,500 staff.** *(Nick Catford)*

CENTRE **Area 8 at 'Burlington' showing the 40-position GPO telephone switchboard that was capable of handling both domestic and international calls.** *(Nick Catford)*

but, by the beginning of the next decade, the government of the day refused to allocate further funds for upgrading and refurbishment. With just a skeleton maintenance staff, the bunker was kept on standby. Even this proved to be too much and, since 2005 or so, the site has been emptied of its fuel and food supplies and has now been decommissioned.

Since the end of the Cold War, underground facilities for the government have been provided beneath the MoD headquarters in Whitehall. Code-named 'Pindar', and described as the 'current contingencies task room', construction began in 1987. The complex was completed in 1994 at a cost of £126.3 million, and provides accommodation for around 100 politicians, military staff and others, with tunnels said to connect the bunker with Downing Street and the Cabinet Office. Alongside the facilities that one might expect to find in such a building, there are hardened communications links with the permanent joint headquarters at Northwood, and a broadcasting studio that would allow the government to address the survivors of whatever crisis had driven the leaders underground.

Regional government facilities

Assuming that nuclear warfare with the Soviet Union was inevitable, the Civil Defence Act 1948 divided mainland Britain into 12 regions, each of which would have its own purpose-built war room or bunker; a single room was provided in Northern Ireland. These facilities could remain in contact with the central war room in London as well as with other civil and military establishments during times of crisis. Construction of the facilities began in 1953, with the last completed in 1956, and, aside from those at Newcastle and London,

BELOW **Dating from the early 1950s, and located at the rear of the government offices in Brooklands Avenue, Cambridge war room was a two-storey surface building; other similar war rooms were semi-sunken.** *(Historic England)*

the buildings were designed to a common pattern, with access provided via a purpose-built reinforced concrete structure on the surface. The Newcastle war room was constructed in an existing underground bunker (see Table 12, page 117).

In 1956, plans were prepared to construct a system of subregional control centres (SRC) from which rescue operations could be co-ordinated following an attack, but little actual progress was made.

The development of the thermonuclear hydrogen bomb brought with it the possibility of a change in tactics; a drawn-out war of attrition was far less likely since the enormous power of the hydrogen bomb would allow an attacker to devastate major centres of population in a shorter campaign. If central government were effectively wiped out in such an attack, then control would pass to a series of regional commissioners, each with the power to replace broad functions of the government in his or her region. As before, there were 12 regions, each with its own regional seat of government (RSG) – sometimes described as a joint civil–

ABOVE Like the war room at Cambridge, the facility at Cheadle was also a two-storey surface design. The building functioned as a SCR until 1968 and later served as the Greater Manchester emergency centre. *(Nick Catford)*

RIGHT Floor plan of a typical two-storey war room. *(Bill Padden)*

BELOW Interior view of Brislington war room; the bunker was abandoned in 1982. *(Nick Catford)*

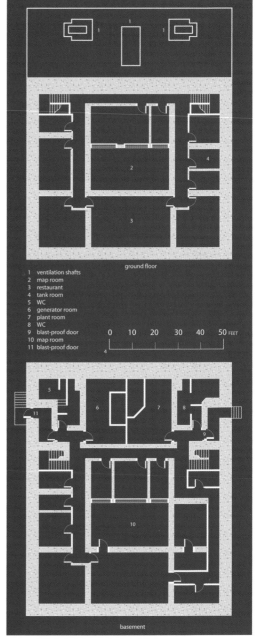

ground floor

1   ventilation shafts
2   map room
3   restaurant
4   tank room
5   WC
6   generator room
7   plant room
8   WC
9   blast-proof door
10 map room
11 blast-proof door

0   10   20   30   40   50 FEET

basement

TABLE 12 LOCATION OF WAR ROOMS AND REGIONAL SEATS OF GOVERNMENT

Region		Location	
		War room	Regional seat of government
RSG 1	Northern	Newcastle	Catterick
RSG 2	North Eastern	Leeds	York
RSG 3	North Midlands	Nottingham	Nottingham
RSG 4	Eastern	Cambridge	Cambridge
RSG 5	London	Chislehurst; Mill Hill; North Cheam; Southall; Wanstead Flats	Chislehurst; Mill Hill; North Cheam; Southall; Wanstead Flats
RSG 6	Southern	Reading	Warren Row
RSG 7	South Western	Brislington (Bristol)	Salcombe
RSG 8	Wales	Cardiff	Brecon
RSG 9	Midlands	Shirley	Kidderminster
RSG 10	North Western	Cheadle (Manchester)	Preston
RSG 11	Northern Ireland	Belfast	Armagh
RSG 12	South Eastern	Tunbridge Wells	Dover
–	Scotland, eastern zone	Kirknewton	Kirknewton
–	Scotland, northern zone	Kirknewton	Anstruther
–	Scotland, western zone	Kirknewton	East Kilbride

TABLE 13 LOCATION OF REGIONAL GOVERNMENT HEADQUARTERS

Region		Location	Notes
RGHQ 1	Scotland, north zone	Anstruther	Former SRHQ and 'Rotor' station
	Scotland, north zone	Cultybraggan	Purpose-built, 1990, replaced Anstruther
	Scotland, east zone	Kirknewton	Former regional war room
	Scotland, west zone	East Kilbride	Former anti-aircraft operations room
	Scotland, central zone	Edinburgh	Former 'Rotor' station
RGHQ 2.1	North Eastern	Shipton	Former 'Rotor' station
RGHQ 2.2		Hexham	Former cold store
RGHQ 3.1	East Midlands	Skendleby	Former 'Rotor' station
RGHQ 3.2		Loughborough	Former cold store
RGHQ 4.1	Eastern	Bawburgh	Former 'Rotor' station
RGHQ 4.2		Hertford	Reinforced basement of government building
RGHQ 4.2		Bedford	Former ROC control centre, replaced Hertford
RGHQ 5.1	London	Kelvedon Hatch	Former 'Rotor' station
RGHQ 6.1	Southern	Dover	WW2 tunnels
RGHQ 6.1		Crowborough	Purpose-built, 1990, replaced Dover
RGHQ 6.2		Basingstoke	Reinforced basement of government building
RGHQ 7.1	South Western	Bolt Head/Ullenwood	Former SRC
RGHQ 7.2		Hope Cove	Former 'Rotor' station and SRC
RGHQ 7.2		Chilmark	Purpose-built, 1988, replaced Ullenwood
RGHQ 8.1	Wales	Llandudno Junction	Former cold store; work abandoned before completion
RGHQ 8.1		Wrexham	Former ROC control centre
RGHQ 8.2		Brackla Hill	Former underground explosives magazine
RGHQ 9.1	West Midlands	Swynnerton	Former ordnance factory and SRC
RGHQ 9.2		Drakelow Tunnels	Former underground factory and SRC
RGHQ 10.1	North Western	Goosnargh	Former ROC facility and SRC
RGHQ 10.2		Hack Green	Former 'Rotor' station
RGHQ 11	Northern Ireland	Belfast	Former regional war room
		Ballymena	Purpose-built, 1990, replaced Belfast

ABOVE RSG 12 at Brooklands Avenue, Cambridge. *(Historic England)*

BELOW The RSG for eastern Scotland was located at Kirknewton, Midlothian. *(Nick Catford)*

BOTTOM Operations room of RSG 2 at York. *(Historic England)*

military headquarters – with some constructed at former war room locations. It was obvious that it was all but impossible to provide protection against the blast or heat produced by a thermonuclear weapon, and, although the buildings were of windowless concrete construction, the structure was intended to render protection from fallout rather than blast, so were not bunkers in the accepted sense.

In June 1963, *Hansard* recorded that the role of the commissioner was to 'enable succour and relief to be brought to the public after an attack … and to marshal services and supplies for essential survival'. This change in approach required a much larger staff, with each commissioner likely to be supported by over 300 people, including 100 military personnel, together with staff from the various ministries, a public information unit, police, fire services, civil defence and communications.

Although supposedly highly confidential, the existence of the RSGs, and their purpose, became common knowledge in February 1963 when members of a group called Spies for Peace broke into the buildings at Warren Row (RSG 6) and removed various documents. Using this material, the group produced a controversial document entitled 'Danger! Official Secret', describing the layout of RSG 6, and pointing out that the government had constructed a series of bunkers that would protect, at the most, 5,000 people, and was carefully planning for the inevitability of a nuclear conflict. Between 3,000 and 4,000 copies of the leaflet were sent to selected members of the press and public in time for distribution during the Easter march organised by the CND. As a result of this information, a group broke away from the march and demonstrated outside the buildings at Warren Row. Predictable public outrage followed, but none of the 'spies' were ever caught.

From 1962 onwards, the RSG were supplemented by what were described as subregional headquarters (SRHQ), the thinking being that each of the 12 regions would be subdivided into 3 subregions, and each of these allocated a purpose-built fallout bunker large enough to accommodate around 300 staff. By 1966, it was recognised that the RSGs would form a prime target for Soviet missiles and the SRHQs and their subregions were promoted

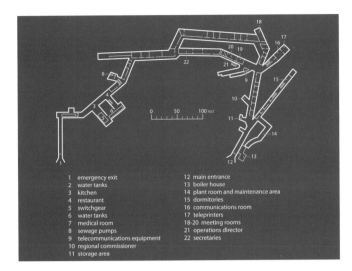

1 emergency exit
2 water tanks
3 kitchen
4 restaurant
5 switchgear
6 water tanks
7 medical room
8 sewage pumps
9 telecommunications equipment
10 regional commissioner
11 storage area
12 main entrance
13 boiler house
14 plant room and maintenance area
15 dormitories
16 communications room
17 teleprinters
18-20 meeting rooms
21 operations director
22 secretaries

ABOVE In 1963, RSG 6 at Warren Row was compromised by a group describing itself as Spies for Peace. The group published details of the installation, including a diagram of the facilities. *(Bill Padden)*

RIGHT Floor plan of a typical RSG, in this case based on RSG 4 at Cambridge. *(Bill Padden)*

BELOW Floor plan of typical RGHQ, based on the purpose-built facilities of RGHQ 7.2 at Chilmark. *(Bill Padden)*

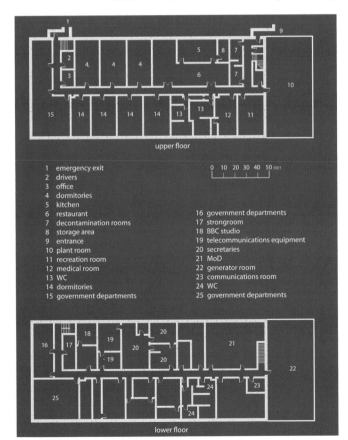

upper floor

1 emergency exit
2 drivers
3 office
4 dormitories
5 kitchen
6 restaurant
7 decontamination rooms
8 storage area
9 entrance
10 plant room
11 recreation room
12 medical room
13 WC
14 dormitories
15 government departments
16 government departments
17 strongroom
18 BBC studio
19 telecommunications equipment
20 secretaries
21 MoD
22 generator room
23 communications room
24 WC
25 government departments

lower floor

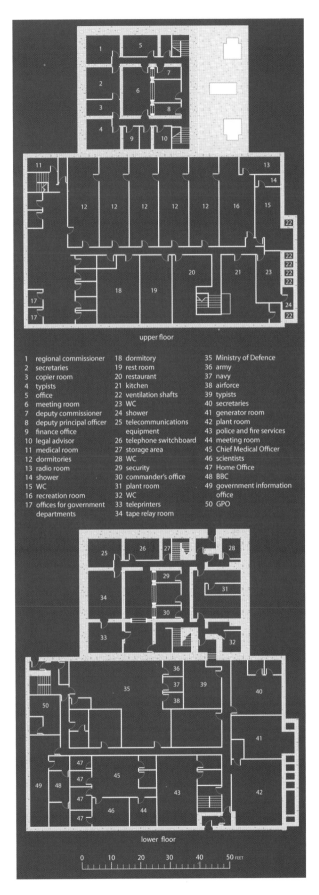

upper floor

1 regional commissioner
2 secretaries
3 copier room
4 typists
5 office
6 meeting room
7 deputy commissioner
8 deputy principal officer
9 finance office
10 legal advisor
11 medical room
12 dormitories
13 radio room
14 shower
15 WC
16 recreation room
17 offices for government departments
18 dormitory
19 rest room
20 restaurant
21 kitchen
22 ventilation shafts
23 WC
24 shower
25 telecommunications equipment
26 telephone switchboard
27 storage area
28 WC
29 security
30 commander's office
31 plant room
32 WC
33 teleprinters
34 tape relay room
35 Ministry of Defence
36 army
37 navy
38 airforce
39 typists
40 secretaries
41 generator room
42 plant room
43 police and fire services
44 meeting room
45 Chief Medical Officer
46 scientists
47 Home Office
48 BBC
49 government information office
50 GPO

lower floor

as the highest echelon of regional government both during the build-up to, and following, a nuclear conflict. Some of the former RSG buildings were reallocated a role as SRCs.

A new plan emerged following the Home Defence Review undertaken by the Thatcher government in 1980, with the establishment of 17 regional government headquarters (RGHQ), housed in new underground buildings, or in refurbished SRC facilities. Towards the end of the decade, three new bunkers were constructed at Chilmark, Crowborough and Cultybraggan, at a cost reputed to be around £80 million each.

The end of the Cold War brought this particular line of thinking to an end, and the bunkers have subsequently been closed. A number have been demolished, but several have been sold to private buyers to be turned into storage facilities, museums and tourist attractions.

County and local authority facilities

In that great British tradition often described as 'muddling through', the organisation of emergency government and civil defence facilities at the county and local authority levels was fragmented and often heavily reliant on volunteers. A new realism seemed to emerge following the Cuban Missile Crisis of 1962, and the Home Defence Review of 1965 empowered local councils to organise, as best they could, following an attack, before devolving power upwards should the situation eventually stabilise.

1 entrance
2 dormitory
3 dormitory
4 medical room
5 water tank
6 WC
7 showers
8 WC
9 kitchen
10 restaurant
11 radio room
12 government departments
13 recreation room
14 entrance
15 underground connecting passage

0 10 20 30 40 50 FEET

16 communications officer
17 telephone switchboard
18 telecommunications equipment
19 MoD
20 regional commissioner
21 principal officer
22 WC
23 switchgear
24 exit
25 generator room
26 meeting room
27 information room
28 entrance
29 government departments
30 secretaries
31 registry
32 scientists
33 communications room
34 mezzanine level
35 plant room
36 air outlet duct

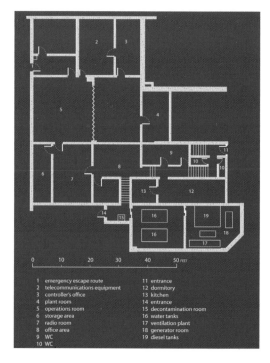

0 10 20 30 40 50 FEET

1 emergency escape route
2 telecommunications equipment
3 controller's office
4 plant room
5 operations room
6 storage area
7 radio room
8 office area
9 WC
10 WC
11 entrance
12 dormitory
13 kitchen
14 entrance
15 decontamination room
16 water tanks
17 ventilation plant
18 generator room
19 diesel tanks

Since 1963, county councils had been obliged to provide a protected bunker large enough to accommodate a staff of up to 80 persons, which could serve as a headquarters during the period of crisis following an attack. The nature of these facilities varied from one authority to another, with some being purpose-built at considerable cost and others, for example, constructed in the basement of the county hall or library. From 1971, county councils were obliged to establish two protected bunkers, with one able to take over from the other if circumstances dictated.

During the last decade of the Cold War, district councils, utilities and nationalised industries were encouraged to construct emergency bunkers to supplement the county structure. In 1987, as part of this scheme, the Home Office was prepared to provide 100% funding for approved bunkers and for other emergency facilities. The end of the Cold War meant that many such bunkers were started but never finished.

Communications facilities

As part of the post-1948 civil defence programme, the government commissioned the General Post Office (GPO), at the time the sole provider of telecommunications throughout most of the country, to develop a hardened trunk-cable network, able to survive anything short of a direct hit. The network was designed to operate alongside the military defence communications network and the government control network, both of which already included hardened telephone exchanges. It would allow the various underground government centres to maintain communication regardless of what unfolded outside, and would connect the major administrative, communications and strategic sites, and handle the data generated by 'Rotor' sites. At the same time, the GPO also established a series of 'area war groups' to assist in integrating the various communications systems into a coherent whole following an attack, so that the public telephone network could be made available for military and administrative traffic. A euphemistically described 'preference system', installed at all telephone exchanges, would cut off 90–98%

of all public telephone subscribers during a crisis, in order to ensure that sufficient capacity remained available for authorised users.

New trunk cables were laid between Glasgow and London, via Manchester and Birmingham, and between London and Bristol, with the latter eventually extended to connect to the transatlantic network. Cables were also rerouted around major cities to reduce their vulnerability in the event of an attack. New 'bomb-proof' telephone exchanges were planned, deep underground, in the centres of Birmingham, Bristol, Glasgow, London and Manchester; there was also a government trunk exchange at Corsham. Three of the new exchanges were completed by the end of 1958, although work on those at Glasgow and Bristol was never finished. Three more trunk exchanges were constructed during the 1960s, at Cambridge, Reading and Tunbridge Wells, designed to help handle traffic from London and to increase reliability during time of war.

Whilst the new trunk exchanges in Birmingham, Manchester and London were being constructed, a series of eight hardened 'intermediate carrier repeater stations' were incorporated at strategic points on the network, designed to boost the signal strength and counteract losses due to the lengths of copper cable involved. The repeater stations were located at Birmingham (two stations), Bristol, Glasgow, Leeds, Manchester (two stations) and Portsmouth. Built partly underground, these repeater stations were constructed from thick concrete with blast-proof doors, and stand-by

ABOVE The London Borough of Lambeth built an 18-room underground bunker into the basement of Pear Tree House on the council's Central Hill Estate. The facility was completed in 1966, but is currently unused. *(Nick Catford)*

ABOVE **Exterior view of the hardened telephone exchange at RAF Upper Heyford.** *(Historic England)*

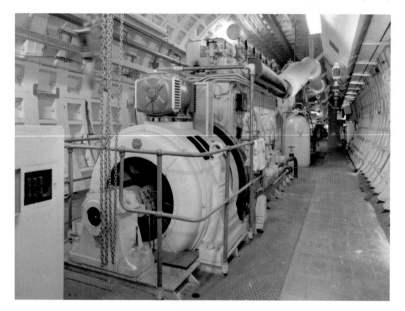

generators were installed for use in the event of a failure of the public supply network.

By the end of the 1950s, the new hardened exchanges, the repeater stations and trunk cables were becoming redundant due to the development of the GPO microwave system. Although promoted to the public as a means of broadcasting television signals, the microwave system was initially considered to be a vital defence asset which would be largely immune to nuclear attack. Under the code name 'Backbone', the system consisted of a chain of 14 stations connecting south-east England to Scotland, designed to provide resilient 'line-of-sight' radio-relay connection between key government, military and civil defence locations.

In the mid-1960s, the GPO microwave system was supplemented by a defence-only network connecting all of the military radar stations and supporting the 'Linesman' air-defence system.

BELOW **The Guardian underground telephone exchange at George Street, Manchester, was one of five similar facilities constructed in the early 1950s to provide hardened communications in the event of a nuclear war. Taken in 1998, this view shows the 80-inch (2.03m) diameter cable tunnels.** *(Historic England)*

ABOVE **One of three Ruston & Hornsby 500kVA generator sets installed at the Kingsway underground trunk exchange in London. The generators maintain services in the event of a mains failure.** *(Nick Catford)*

RIGHT **Typical floor plan for a GPO PR2 protected repeater station. These stations were designed to boost the signal strength of telephone calls, and to counteract losses due to the lengths of copper cable involved.** *(Bill Padden)*

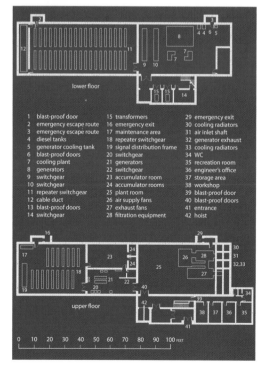

lower floor

1 blast-proof door	15 transformers	29 emergency exit
2 emergency escape route	16 emergency exit	30 cooling radiators
3 emergency escape route	17 maintenance area	31 air inlet shaft
4 diesel tanks	18 repeater switchgear	32 generator exhaust
5 generator cooling tank	19 signal distribution frame	33 cooling radiators
6 blast-proof doors	20 switchgear	34 WC
7 cooling plant	21 generators	35 recreation room
8 generators	22 switchgear	36 engineer's office
9 switchgear	23 accumulator room	37 storage area
10 switchgear	24 accumulator rooms	38 workshop
11 repeater switchgear	25 plant room	39 blast-proof door
12 cable duct	26 air supply fans	40 blast-proof doors
13 blast-proof doors	27 exhaust fans	41 entrance
14 switchgear	28 filtration equipment	42 hoist

upper floor

0 10 20 30 40 50 60 70 80 90 100 FEET

Emergency control trains

It is also worth mentioning special railway rolling stock that each of the British Rail regions held, which were described as 'emergency control trains (mobile communications centres)', and intended to allow the government to tap into the telephone network in the event of nuclear war. The Southern Region, for example, had two such trains, consisting of three-coach sets converted from stock that dated back to the 1930s: the carriages were sufficiently narrow to be able to be moved to anywhere on the railway system and remained in service from the early 1960s to the early 1980s.

Fuel and pipeline systems

It is an inescapable truth that mechanised warfare, whether on land or in the air, demands virtually limitless availability of fuel. This fact had been well understood by those planning the invasion of Normandy, and, as early as 1942, work had started on the development of a 1,000-mile (1,600km) long pipeline system, together with relay pumping stations, to connect the refinery and storage facilities at Liverpool and Bristol to a terminal at Shanklin Chine on the Isle of Wight. From here, the first pipeline to France – part of the 'pipeline under the ocean' (PLUTO) project – was laid on 12 August 1944, pumping fuel to Cherbourg. Between August 1944 and May 1945, over 172 million gallons (780 million litres) of fuel were pumped to France. Recognising the importance of the scheme, General Eisenhower is on record as having said that: 'second in daring only to the Mulberry Harbours, was PLUTO' for its contribution in winning the war in Europe.

After the war ended, much of the undersea pipework was recovered and scrapped for its metal content. However, the basic infrastructure of underground pipelines, terminals, refineries and pumping stations was retained, together with six coastal fuel depots. In the post-war years, the primary purpose of this system, which came to be described as the Government Pipeline and Storage System (GPSS), was to provide a means of moving aviation fuel around the country, and, during the 1950s, the system was extended to around 1,250 miles (2,000km) of underground,

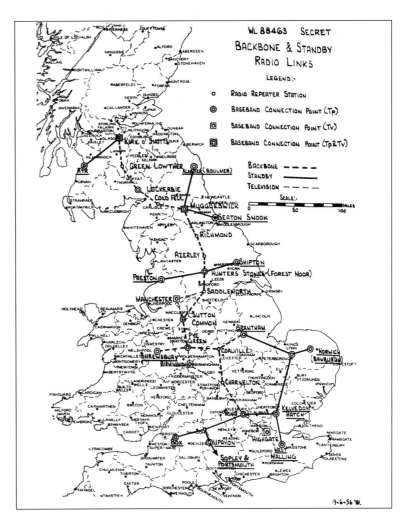

ABOVE As proposed in 1956, the 'Backbone' communications system was to comprise a chain of 14 stations connecting south-east England to Scotland, providing 'line-of-sight' radio-relay connection between key government, military and civil defence locations. *(Warehouse Collection)*

LEFT The route of the government pipeline system is indicated on the surface by white posts with small black-and-yellow striped 'roofs'. *(Oil and Pipelines Agency)*

gallons (45 million litres) of petrol and diesel fuel for road vehicles, with around 10% of these totals used by the military. The same network of pipes was used for all of the different fuels and contamination was kept to a minimum by managing the sequence in which fuels were despatched: the sequence running from the lightest (naphtha) to the heaviest (diesel) and back to the lightest; inflatable spheres were also used to separate different 'parcels' of fuel.

Following a detailed impact assessment, in May 2012, the government announced its intention to sell the GPSS to the highest bidder. The process was overseen by investment bankers Rothschild, with the Spanish company Compañía Logística de Hidrocarburos (CLH) eventually making a payment of £82m for the pipeline and 46 related facilities in the spring of 2015; the naval fuel depots were not included in the sale. A contract drawn up between the MoD and CLH covered the continued military use of the system.

Provisions stores

A nuclear strike on Britain, where something like 80% of the population live in urban areas, would have a devastating impact on day-to-day life and on the maintenance of law and order. Worse still, Britain imports up to 40% of the nation's food requirement and a full-scale nuclear attack would see these imports dry up immediately as ships turned away from British ports. Hunger riots would be inevitable.

The government had always assumed that, for the first few days following an attack, the population in affected areas would be able to survive using their own resources. In the widely discredited Home Office publication 'Protect and Survive', published in 1980, the population was advised that two weeks' food supply should be laid-in during the build-up to a nuclear crisis – although contemporary research showed that few members of the public seemed to have any idea how much food was required for a family to survive for two weeks. There was far less reliance on domestic cold-storage in the 1950s and '60s, and many more canned goods were available, but, if the electricity- and fuel-supply networks were destroyed, anything that was stored in freezers or refrigerators would quickly spoil. And, to make matters worse, food

cross-country pipework, together with ancillary facilities. The route of the pipework, much of which is buried 6ft (1,800mm) underground, is marked on the surface by white posts with small black-and-yellow striped 'roofs'.

During the late 1950s and '60s, many of the fuel depots, formerly under RAF control, were passed to the Ministry of Power, and later to the MoD. From 1986, the system was operated by the Oil and Pipelines Agency (OPA) on behalf of the MoD, working in conjunction with the Defence Fuels Group. The OPA also had responsibility for six Royal Navy oil fuel depots.

Eventually, all of the RAF's major airfields, including those leased to the USAF, for example at Lakenheath and Mildenhall, were connected. Private use was also encouraged to assist in covering the costs of maintaining and operating the infrastructure, providing it 'did not impinge upon its primary purpose of supplying the required fuel for defence purposes and did not require capital investment from public funds'. All of Britain's major civilian airports were supplied by the system, with something like 40% of aviation fuel carried by the GPSS. By 2009, the system was supplying 145 million gallons (660 million litres) of aviation fuel, 58 million gallons (265 million litres) of marine diesel and 10 million manufacture would cease until raw materials were available, and until the electricity, gas and water utilities were once again operational. At the same time, the bulk supply chain would almost certainly break down due to the difficulties of moving around the country.

Although the scale of any likely devastation was not of the same order, this situation had already been faced during the Second World War when the government had started building and stocking emergency food stores. By the end of the conflict, there were more than 40 huge cold stores, 16 grain silos and dozens of general-purpose stores strategically placed across the country, generally close to a railway line to aid distribution. Construction of emergency storage facilities continued into the post-war years, and, by 1951, the number of storage depots peaked at 260, falling to 136 by the mid-1960s.

During the 1950s, the Ministry of Food filled these depots and cold stores with a stockpile of 745,000 tons of foodstuffs, consisting mainly of corned beef, biscuits, flour, sugar, yeast, dried milk and other raw materials ready for processing. By the end of the decade, the quantity had fallen to 582,500 tons. However, it was clear that, regardless of how much the government managed to store, food would rapidly become a scarce commodity following a nuclear attack and rationing would become inevitable. On the basis that a starving population was unlikely to be compliant, the government would eventually have to take control of all food supplies, identifying and requisitioning large stocks of basic commodities, including animal feeds and agricultural fertilisers.

The supply of food to the public after an attack would have been administered by the RGHQ, from the bulk stocks held in government storage, from central stocks held in commercial supply warehouses and from food producers and farms, with regard to the need for future agricultural production once any recovery was under way. Emergency powers were available for local controllers to requisition any remaining, undamaged stocks held in shops and commercial warehouses.

However, the Home Office acknowledged that the food stockpiles were, nevertheless, 'insufficient to meet the needs of the surviving population over a protracted period', whilst

failing to propose a long-term solution beyond an expressed desire to 're-orientate towards subsistence agriculture growing more food crops, particularly cereal'. But the effects of any attack on agriculture would depend, not only on the severity and scope of the attack itself, but also on the time of year. An attack in late autumn would mean that the year's harvest had already been gathered, whilst an attack in spring would affect vulnerable crops that were still growing. The standard Home Office attack scenario of the period assumed a distributed yield of 200 megatons, and an analysis of the effects of such an attack by the Ministry of Agriculture, Fisheries and Food suggested that 27,000 square miles (70,000km²) of mainland Britain, some 30% of the total land area, would be seriously affected by radiation to the extent that crop production would be compromised, and agricultural yields would fall by a significant amount. No effective solution was ever proposed, and it seems that partial starvation of survivors would have been the order of the day.

Many of the cold stores were disposed of during the 1970s, and all of the food stocks were sold or destroyed within five years of the end of the Cold War.

BELOW Located beside the railway at Haughley, the Stowmarket grain silo was constructed in 1954 and demolished in 2008; the site is now a concrete works. The silo was designed by Eric Bedford of the Ministry of Works; a similar facility was constructed at Ely. *(Historic England)*

Chapter Eight

Civil defence

In May 1980, the Home Office published a booklet purporting to instruct the British public on 'how to make your home and your family as safe as possible under nuclear attack'. Entitled *Protect and Survive*, its foreword explained that the booklet would be distributed free to every household as part of a public information campaign if the country were to be faced by 'an immediate threat of nuclear war'. For those who preferred to read the advice before such a time, it was available for purchase for a modest 50 pence – at that time roughly the price of a half-pint of lager.

OPPOSITE Public shelters were never built in Britain, but in the USA the government had a somewhat different approach. Constructed in 1961, with a capacity of 1,000, the Highlands Community Fallout Shelter, at Boise, Idaho, was the first prototype community fallout shelter in the USA. *(US Office of Civil Defense)*

'It must be frankly recognised that there is at present no means of providing adequate protection for the people of this country against nuclear attack.'

British Government Defence White Paper, 1957

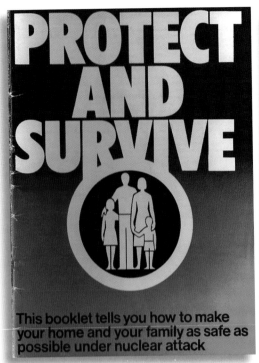

RIGHT The booklet *Protect and Survive* was published by HMSO in May 1980 and was intended to inform the public on how to protect themselves during a nuclear attack. Highly critical of the government message, the CND produced its own publication entitled *Civil Defence: The Cruellest Confidence Trick*. (Warehouse Collection)

FAR RIGHT The US government also published information booklets intended to assuage the fears of the public. This example, titled *Survival under Atomic Attack*, dates from 1950. (Warehouse Collection)

Two years later, in 1982, Duncan Campbell, a staff writer on *New Statesman* published a blistering exposé of civil defence planning in Britain. Entitled *War Plan UK*, Campbell's book explained that the priority was to protect the government and its ability to continue to fight the war, and, at the same time, to suppress signs of dissent in the population. Following five years'

research, and drawing on anonymous inside sources and material that, at the time, were not in the public domain, Campbell suggested that the public was being deceived. He explained that, despite years of often misguided and ineffective planning, waste and misinformation, there were no credible plans for protecting the population, no public shelters had been constructed, and there would be scant medical aid for what would inevitably be hundreds of thousands of injured and dying. The picture that Campbell paints is not a pretty one.

Campbell's bleak and often angry account may not be correct in every detail, but we must assume that it bears a close relation to the truth. Copies of the book can still be found through rare book dealers, and the author's current website is also worth a visit (www.duncancampbell.org).

Certainly, much of the advice given in *Protect and Survive*, as well as in a 1963 Her Majesty's Stationary Office (HMSO) civil defence booklet entitled *Advising the Householder on Protection against Nuclear Attack*, borders on the ridiculous. Despite warning that the 'explosion of an H-bomb would cause total destruction several miles around', the authors suggested that householders could provide protection for a meaningful period by bricking-up windows, sandbagging the staircase or digging an underground chamber lined with timber.

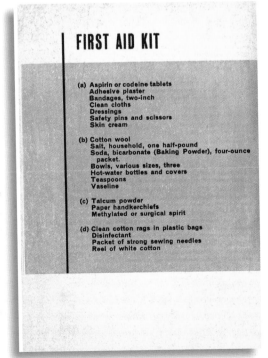

RIGHT List of items for a basic household first-aid kit that appeared in the 1963 HMSO booklet, *Advising the Householder on Protection against Nuclear Attack*. (Warehouse Collection)

However, despite a somewhat ambivalent attitude towards the civilian population, perhaps arising out of the scale of the problem, civil defence formed an intrinsic part of the government's Cold War strategy. Much of the planning subsequently proved to be naïve and misguided, or, as in the case of the plan to construct large-scale shelters, simply too expensive, but it did suggest to the population that it might be possible to survive nuclear war. The advent of the hydrogen bomb changed all this. The sheer scale of any likely attack, and the devastating aftermath, made nonsense of any government plans. There was a reluctance to come clean about this, but, by 1968, the Civil Defence Corps had been stood down and the government's civil defence plan could best be described as 'stay put', arguing that 'no one part of the United Kingdom will be safer than any other'. This is undoubtedly true, although, regardless of the reasons in favour of evacuation, there was simply nowhere for the population to go.

If the British government can be accused of failing to plan for the protection of the civilian population in the event of a nuclear attack, it is almost certainly because no amount of planning could possibly mitigate the effects of such an event. Even as late as 1987 the World Health Organization (WHO) was saying that 'the plight of survivors would be physically and psychologically appalling'. The dishonesty lies in attempts that were made over the years to deceive the public into believing that it might be possible to survive and, even, to rebuild the nation.

'Four-minute warning'

Since almost the beginning of the Cold War, the idea of the 'four-minute warning' has entered into the public consciousness. In practice, it was likely that any warning of impending nuclear attack issued to the public would be of three minutes or less, but whether it was three or four minutes long, the warning was of little practical value. Undeterred, in 1957, the Home Office established the United Kingdom Warning and Monitoring Organisation (UKWMO) to provide the civil and military authorities, and the public, with warning of a likely attack. A UKWMO leaflet boasted that

'ten million lives may have been saved' by early warnings, though it is not clear how or where.

The UKWMO was also tasked with providing details of any subsequent nuclear strikes, together with an assessment of the path and intensity of associated fallout, using a network of 870 monitoring posts across the country. There was conflict between the Home Office and the RAF about who was actually in charge of the warning system, but, regardless, any warning would have been issued by a UKWMO officer located at Strike Command's Operations Centre nuclear bunker at RAF High Wycombe – or elsewhere in the event that circumstances had removed High Wycombe from the equation.

The warning equipment was code-named 'Handel', and consisted of speech-broadcast and siren-control systems, linking High Wycombe to about 250 police stations. Construction had started in 1960, and two separate networks were used, routed to avoid likely target areas. If an incoming attack were detected, the operator would press a red button – Cold War buttons always seem to be red – and make a verbal announcement to indicate the nature of the alert. Three levels of warning were defined: 'attack warning, red' indicated that an attack was imminent; a 'grey' warning indicated that fallout was expected within the hour; and 'black', that fallout was expected immediately. The approved announcement for the all-clear was 'attack message, white'.

High-frequency carrier signals were used to transmit the warning to police stations over the speaking-clock network, and the warnings would also have been sent to the BBC Wartime Broadcasting Service by telephone link. The air-raid sirens were operated automatically, with the familiar rising and falling wail indicating a 'red warning', urging the public to seek cover immediately; in Scotland, the warning was apparently to be delivered by 'whistle' rather than siren. The 'grey' warning, which had been discontinued by the late 1960s, consisted of an interrupted steady tone, whilst the 'black' warning consisted of three pyrotechnic maroons fired in quick succession. The all-clear was a steady note.

Under the provisions of the Broadcasting Act 1980, the government assumed the legal right to take editorial control of radio and television channels in the event of a national emergency.

BELOW Broadcast facilities at Hack Green RGHQ, now preserved as part of a Cold War museum. *(Warehouse Collection)*

Television and radio broadcasts, warning of the impending attack and the dangers of fallout, would have been made at regular intervals from the Wartime Broadcasting Service using a special studio at Broadcasting House; fully equipped studios were also provided in

many of the RSG. During the first 12 hours after the attack, the programme would have been broadcast every two hours on all radio and TV frequencies set aside for the BBC, and the actual script of the warning has recently been released. It begins: 'This is the Wartime Broadcasting Service. This country has been attacked with nuclear weapons. Communications have been severely disrupted, and the number of casualties and the extent of the damage are not yet known. We shall bring you further information as soon as possible. Meanwhile, stay tuned to this wavelength, stay calm and stay in your own homes.'

Following the end of the Cold War, the UKWMO was stood down in November 1992.

Public information

In 1957, HMSO produced its first publication intended to alert the public to the horrors of nuclear warfare, and like most of the similar publications that followed, it was both sketchy and upbeat, not an easy feat bearing in mind the subject matter. Entitled *The Hydrogen Bomb* and priced at a modest 2.5p, the 32-page publication was described as 'a comprehensive pamphlet on nuclear weapons and their effects … [including] the facts about the hydrogen bomb'. The pamphlet described the nature of a nuclear explosion, as well as detailing the effects of the resulting fireball and blast, and the dangers of radiation. Charming illustrations showed a well-dressed couple, complete with small child, taking refuge under their stairs or in an earth-covered slit trench, and there were the usual platitudes about civil defence and the saving of 'millions of lives'. Readers who were keen to learn more were directed to the *Manual of Civil Defence: Pamphlet Number 1: Nuclear Weapons*, where the information was considerably more technical and factual. This had replaced a previous publication, dated 1950, entitled *Civil Defence: Manual of Basic Training, Volume II: Atomic Warfare*.

In 1958, taking advice from various relevant bodies, HMSO published a pamphlet for farmers giving information about the effects of radioactive fallout on crops and the land. *Home Defence and the Farmer* purported to 'suggest in general terms how livestock and crops could

ABOVE With more than 3,000 examples constructed between 1953 and 1956, the 'Green Goddess' was well equipped for its civil defence role, carrying a Sigmund FN5 pump with a capacity of 900–1,000 gallons (4,100–4,500 litres) per minute, together with a wide range of rescue equipment. Many of these vehicles remained in Home Office stores until 2005. *(Warehouse Collection)*

RIGHT Commer Q4 transportable water unit generally known as the 'Bikini' truck. The vehicle held three inflatable rafts and nine lightweight pumps; each raft carried three of the pumps and was designed to allow water to be pumped from inland lakes or rivers that were inaccessible to conventional pumps and appliances. *(Warehouse Collection)*

long-term storage where they remained for another 20 years. There was a significant sale of all kinds of kit in April 1989, but many of the Land Rovers, Austin Gipsies and 'Green Goddesses', often showing extremely low mileage, were retained at Marchington Camp, near Uttoxeter, where they were maintained and regularly exercised during their long years in storage. They were gradually disposed of over the following years, although several of the 'Green Goddesses' were retained until 2005, when the last 900 examples were sold, many with all of the on-board equipment.

RIGHT Fordson Thames ET6 civil defence rescue section vehicle. *(Warehouse Collection)*

Aftermath

At Hiroshima, a single nuclear blast estimated at just 15 kilotons is believed to have killed 70–80,000, with roughly half the deaths occurring within 24 hours of the blast; a further 69,000 were injured, and deaths from the effects of heat flash and radiation continued for many years. The second bomb, with a yield of 21 kilotons, was dropped on Nagasaki, resulting in the deaths of 75,000 people, with a further 75,000 injured. The numbers of people affected, in even a small way, are huge, and, even as late as 1977, more than 350,000

people were still registered as *hibakusha* – meaning they were exposed to the effects of the bombs. By 2014, the number had only fallen to 192,719. Uncertain though they may be, these figures are the only tangible data that is available to estimate the effects of a full-scale nuclear war and, not surprisingly, predictions for the numbers likely to be killed and injured vary wildly (see Table 14, page 141).

In March 1955, a report by Sir William Strath, then head of the Cabinet Office Central War Plans Secretariat and leader of the Strath Committee, laid out a stark assessment of whether Britain could survive a thermonuclear attack from the Soviet Union. Strath postulated that a night attack on the major centres of population using ten 10-megaton fusion weapons would create 'utter devastation', killing 12 million people and seriously injuring or disabling a further 4 million: in other words, around one-third of the then population of the country would be affected. Heat and blast would account for the majority of the casualties, causing some 9 million deaths, with less than 3 million killed by radiation.

Strath addressed post-conflict government policy under three headings: life-saving, national survival and national recovery. He pointed out that huge sums of money would be required to save lives – sums of money that

PRESIDENT
KENNEDY
BE
CAREFUL

PEACE
or
Perish

THE
UN
HANDLE
THE
CUBAN
CRISIS!

ce your
esponsibilit
and give US

Peace

of the world's population were unhappy about living with the continual threat of nuclear warfare and, as atmospheric testing became almost commonplace, anti-war movements began to emerge across the world. In Europe, organisations such as the British Peace

Committee and the Direct Action Committee (DAC) Against Nuclear War started to organise protest rallies. The CND was launched at a public meeting in London in February 1958, and, although often associated with left-wing politics, it appealed to all sectors of society, including prominent scientists, academics, religious leaders, journalists, writers, actors and musicians. Advocating a policy of unilateral nuclear disarmament for Britain, the first visible CND action was its support of the DAC Easter 1958 march from London to Aldermaston; from 1959, the march was organised by CND, with marchers walking from Aldermaston to London. By the following year some 100,000 people were involved.

The marches continued until 1963 when the international Test-Ban Treaty was signed. Support for CND waned in response to a perceived reduction in the threat of nuclear war, but the marches were revived in the early 1970s and '80s, the latter in response to Margaret Thatcher's agreement in 1979 to allow US cruise missiles to be stationed on British soil. At the forefront of this revitalised movement were the Greenham Common Women's Peace Camp and the Molesworth People's Peace Camp, the latter attracting both men and women. Both became part of a network opposing NATO plans to deploy GLCM and 'Pershing 2' intercontinental ballistic missiles in Europe.

The peace camp at Greenham Common was established in September 1981 when 36 women from a Cardiff-based group called Women for Life on Earth chained themselves to the fence surrounding the base. The protests continued, generating huge media attention – one BBC TV news programme actually suggested that anyone approaching the bunkers in which the missiles were stored would be shot! In April 1983, about 70,000 women formed a 14-mile (23km) human chain from Greenham to Aldermaston and AWE Burghfield where nuclear weapons were made, and, at the end of the year, 50,000 women encircled the base. Although the last missiles left Greenham Common in 1991, the camp remained active for 19 years and was not disbanded until the year 2000.

By the time the cruise missiles were delivered to Greenham Common and Molesworth in

1983, another protest group had emerged, calling itself Cruise Watch. So successful was this group in tracking and harassing the missile convoys whenever they carried out exercises on public roads that the authorities eventually resorted to moving the missiles only at night and under police escort.

'Ban the Bomb' protests were not confined to Britain and Europe. Greenpeace had its origins in attempts to stop the USA from testing at Amchitka, Alaska, in 1971, funding the action through a free concert. The US anti-nuclear movement probably reached its peak in the 1980s, with the actions of the Plowshares Group drawing particular attention. A Plowshares rally in Central Park in 1982 is said to have attracted almost a million protestors, whilst, more recently, in 2012, three activists broke into the nuclear weapons facility at Oak Ridge National Laboratory, causing a temporary shut-down.

The CND (www.cnduk.org) continues its work to the present day, with the focus currently on protest against the replacement of 'Trident', opposition to a nuclear-armed NATO and campaigning for a global ban on nuclear weapons.

ABOVE View of the administration building at RAF Greenham Common, containing the missile command centre from which the launch codes for the cruise missiles would have been broadcast. Greenham Common was home to 96 missiles stored on mobile launcher vehicles. *(Nick Catford)*

BELOW Aerial view of RAF Molesworth showing the protected bunkers in which the cruise missiles were stored. Each bunker consisted of three bays, each housing one MAN tractor, one BGM-109G ground-launched cruise missile TEL semi-trailer and 16 missiles; there were also two launch control centres. *(US Department of Defense)*

'Now is the time to affirm not only the immorality of nuclear weapons but the immorality of their possession, thereby clearing the road to abolition.'

Pope Francis, December 2014